T0384943

An Analysis of

Friedrich Nietzsche's

On the Genealogy of Morality

Don Berry

Published by Macat International Ltd
24:13 Coda Centre, 189 Munster Road, London SW6 6AW.

Distributed exclusively by Routledge
2 Park Square, Milton Park, Abingdon, Oxon OX14 4RN
711 Third Avenue, New York, NY 10017, USA

Routledge is an imprint of the Taylor & Francis Group, an informa business

Copyright © 2017 by Macat International Ltd
Macat International has asserted its right under the Copyright, Designs and Patents Act
1988 to be identified as the copyright holder of this work.

www.macat.com
info@macat.com

Cataloguing in Publication Data
A catalogue record for this book is available from the British Library.
Library of Congress Cataloguing-in-Publication Data is available upon request.
Cover illustration: Capucine Deslouis

ISBN 978-1-912303-10-6 (hardback)
ISBN 978-1-912127-19-1 (paperback)
ISBN 978-1-912281-98-5 (e-book)

Notice

CONTENTS

THE MACAT LIBRARY
The Macat Library is a series of unique academic explorations of
seminal works in the humanities and social sciences – books and
papers that have had a significant and widely recognised impact on
their disciplines. It has been created to serve as much more than just a
summary of what lies between the covers of a great book. It illuminates
and explores the influences on, ideas of, and impact of that book. Our
goal is to offer a learning resource that encourages critical thinking and
fosters a better, deeper understanding of important ideas.

Each publication is divided into three Sections: Influences, Ideas, and
Impact. Each Section has four Modules. These explore every important
facet of the work, and the responses to it.

This Section-Module structure makes a Macat Library book easy to
use, but it has another important feature. Because each Macat book is
written to the same format, it is possible (and encouraged!) to cross-
reference multiple Macat books along the same lines of inquiry or
research. This allows the reader to open up interesting interdisciplinary
pathways.

To further aid your reading, lists of glossary terms and people
mentioned are included at the end of this book (these are indicated by
an asterisk [*] throughout) – as well as a list of works cited.

Macat has worked with the University of Cambridge to identify the
elements of critical thinking and understand the ways in which six
different skills combine to enable effective thinking.
Three allow us to fully understand a problem; three more give us
the tools to solve it. Together, these six skills make up the
PACIER model of critical thinking. They are:

ANALYSIS – understanding how an argument is built
EVALUATION – exploring the strengths and weaknesses of an argument
INTERPRETATION – understanding issues of meaning

CREATIVE THINKING – coming up with new ideas and fresh connections
PROBLEM-SOLVING – producing strong solutions
REASONING – creating strong arguments

To find out more, visit **WWW.MACAT.COM.**

CRITICAL THINKING AND *ON THE GENEALOGY OF MORALITY*

Primary critical thinking skill: INTERPRETATION
Secondary critical thinking skill: CREATIVE THINKING

On the Genealogy of Morality was written in 1887, when Friedrich Nietzsche was at the height of his powers as a philosopher and master of German prose. Here he criticizes the idea that there is just one conception of moral goodness, dissecting the contemporary practice of morality and looking at it from a historical viewpoint. Rather than following a metaphysical or religious approach, Nietzsche adopts a naturalistic framework, which is grounded in history and natural science, to understand our conceptions of good and evil in the Christianized Western world. He also charts the origins of the human conscience back to primitive credit-debtor relationships, and gives a critical discussion of the 'ascetic ideal' wherein the best kind of human life is seen as one of self-denial and abstinence.

Nietzsche ultimately hoped that his "philosophers of the future" would put forward new ideas for reshaping morality so as to allow human beings to flourish, and the text demonstrates the creative, artistic spirit he hoped these new thinkers would adopt. Sartre's existentialism, Freud's psychoanalysis, and Foucault's genealogical histories were all built on the philosophical and methodological ground laid by Nietzsche's work as a whole, and perhaps most of all in *On the Genealogy of Morality.*

ABOUT THE AUTHOR OF THE ORIGINAL WORK

Friedrich Nietzsche (1844–1900) was a German philosopher and scholar of history and classics. Instead of following his father and grandfather into the Church, Nietzsche became a professor of philology (the study of the structure and development of language) at the age of just 24. His approach to philosophy combined historical and classical scholarship with ideas drawn from science. He wrote many books, all of which were almost entirely ignored in his lifetime. Nietzsche left academic life in 1879 and suffered a breakdown in 1889 from which he never recovered. He died in obscurity 11 years later, and his genius was only truly recognized in the twentieth century.

ABOUT THE AUTHOR OF THE ANALYSIS

Dr Don Berry holds a PhD in philosophy from University College London and a MA in mathematics from the University of Cambridge. His research focuses on virtue ethics.

ABOUT MACAT

GREAT WORKS FOR CRITICAL THINKING

Macat is focused on making the ideas of the world's great thinkers accessible and comprehensible to everybody, everywhere, in ways that promote the development of enhanced critical thinking skills.

It works with leading academics from the world's top universities to produce new analyses that focus on the ideas and the impact of the most influential works ever written across a wide variety of academic disciplines. Each of the works that sit at the heart of its growing library is an enduring example of great thinking. But by setting them in context – and looking at the influences that shaped their authors, as well as the responses they provoked – Macat encourages readers to look at these classics and game-changers with fresh eyes. Readers learn to think, engage and challenge their ideas, rather than simply accepting them.

"Macat offers an amazing first-of-its-kind tool for interdisciplinary learning and research. Its focus on works that transformed their disciplines and its rigorous approach, drawing on the world's leading experts and educational institutions, opens up a world-class education to anyone."

Andreas Schleicher
Director for Education and Skills, Organisation for Economic Co-operation and Development

'Macat is taking on some of the major challenges in university education … They have drawn together a strong team of active academics who are producing teaching materials that are novel in the breadth of their approach.'

Prof Lord Broers,
former Vice-Chancellor of the University of Cambridge

'The Macat vision is exceptionally exciting. It focuses upon new modes of learning which analyse and explain seminal texts which have profoundly influenced world thinking and so social and economic development. It promotes the kind of critical thinking which is essential for any society and economy. This is the learning of the future.'

Rt Hon Charles Clarke, former UK Secretary of State for Education

'The Macat analyses provide immediate access to the critical conversation surrounding the books that have shaped their respective discipline, which will make them an invaluable resource to all of those, students and teachers, working in the field.'

Professor William Tronzo, University of California at San Diego

WAYS IN TO THE TEXT

KEY POINTS

- Friedrich Nietzsche was a German philosopher, classical scholar, and cultural critic whose writings exerted a tremendous influence on European intellectual life in the twentieth century.

- In *On the Genealogy of Morality*, Nietzsche calls into question the Judeo-Christian morality then dominant in Europe and considers other possibilities for ethical life.

- Nietzsche's *Genealogy* takes a historical approach to moral philosophy. The book is also highly personal, full of emotively charged rhetoric and engaging poetical imagery.

Who Was Friedrich Nietzsche?

Friedrich Nietzsche, the author of *On the Genealogy of Morality* (1887), was a German philosopher, philologist* (an expert on the historical development of languages), and classical scholar who criticized the values and morality of his age. He had hoped to effect a rejuvenation of what he saw as a declining German culture, which Nietzsche felt lacked artistic direction—for instance, in music, theatre, and opera. Writing after the period of European intellectual history known as the Enlightenment,* when Europe developed the modern tradition of scientific thought, he sought to draw out the consequences of the triumph of Enlightenment secularism—the general agreement that

society should not now be based on religious beliefs and practices—
and to ask whether absolute values were really possible in a world
without God.

Though his writings were largely unknown during his own
lifetime, his work ultimately influenced not only generations of
philosophers, but also poets, novelists, theologians, psychologists, and
even musicians and dancers.

Nietzsche was born in 1844 to a devout family of Lutherans★ (fol-
lowers of a branch of Protestant★ Christian practice founded on the
thought of the German theologian Martin Luther). They lived in the
small town of Röcken in Saxony, Germany. Nietzsche was expected
to enter the Church, but when he went to study theology and
philology* at the University of Bonn in 1864 he swiftly lost interest in
theology. A year later he followed his professor, Friedrich Wilhelm
Ritschl,* to continue studying philology at the University of Leipzig.
Nietzsche was appointed an associate professor of philology at the
University of Basel in 1869 (at the age of just 24) on Ritschl's
recommendation. Ritschl stated unequivocally that he had "never had
such a talented student."[1]

Nietzsche's academic career was cut short when he retired in 1879,
partly for health reasons but also because of his increasing frustration
with his scholarly duties as a professor. He spent the following decade
living a solitary life traveling around France, Germany, Switzerland,
and Italy in pursuit of better health; it was under these conditions of
isolation that he composed *On the Genealogy of Morality* in 1887.
Though he lived until 1900, he suffered a mental breakdown in
January 1889 that left him severely mentally incapacitated for the final
decade of his short but productive life.

What Does *On the Genealogy of Morality* Say?

Nietzsche's *On the Genealogy of Morality* takes the form of an extended
historical narrative that examines the roots of nineteenth-century

European morality, the Judeo-Christian* morality characterized by the ideals of compassion, humility, selflessness, chastity, piety, and truthfulness. By inquiring into the origins of this moral framework, Nietzsche sought to bring its chief values into question, and to ask whether an alternative way of thinking and feeling might enhance our experience of life.

Since this Judeo-Christian morality still influences our ethics and actions today, *Genealogy* retains its importance as a powerful challenge to contemporary values. As the Nietzsche scholar Maudemarie Clark* notes in the introduction to the 1998 edition of *Genealogy*: "Many consider it indispensable reading for understanding the intellectual life of the twentieth century."[2]

The text is divided into three essays, each comprising a history of a single aspect of moral life. The first gives the origins of our current concepts of "good" and "evil." For Nietzsche, these arose when the weak and mediocre masses rose up to take a kind of spiritual revenge on their natural masters: strong, fearless, noble types, who then became regarded as "evil" under the Christian interpretation of morality.

In the second essay, Nietzsche writes a history of the human moral conscience. He locates its origins in more primitive creditor–debtor relationships and in the pleasure gained from inflicting punishment. Here, Nietzsche asserts that as societies become more civilized and physical aggression toward others is less tolerated, our natural instincts to cruelty turn in on ourselves, creating what we now experience as guilt or bad conscience.

Finally, in the third essay he describes the "ascetic ideal" whereby the highest kind of human life is seen as the monastic life of piety, abstinence, and self-denial. Nietzsche attributes the widespread acceptance of this ideal to the fact that no other competing ideals had yet been articulated—though he advances this as an open challenge to his "philosophers of the future" rather than presenting his own alternative to the ascetic ideal.

11

Nietzsche is now a central figure in undergraduate courses in departments that focus on teaching analytic* philosophy (the dominant approach to philosophy in the English speaking world, which stresses clarity, logical argument, and attention to language). In continental* philosophy—a collection of approaches that emphasise lived human experience and historical enquiry—he is perhaps the central figure and has inspired the core questions and methodology of its practitioners.

The text exemplifies a way of doing philosophy that has a basis in history, as Nietzsche makes use of a wealth of concrete examples and sources. This combination of philosophy and historical scholarship was hugely influential in the twentieth century, with important thinkers like the French historian and social theorist Michel Foucault* taking the same approach. Though Nietzsche often wrote in aphorisms-short, pithy sayings that jumped swiftly from one theme to another-*Genealogy* is a more systematic work and so highly suitable for focused study of his thought. It was written near the end of his career, when he was at the height of his intellectual powers, and it deals with the topics that were closest to him. It is therefore an excellent entry point to his writings.

Why Does *On the Genealogy of Morality* Matter?

The morality of contemporary Europe is largely Christian in origin. This morality conceives of the ideal man or woman as compassionate, meek, selfless, humble, chaste, and pious. Yet as Nietzsche shows in *Genealogy*, in other periods of history—such as ancient Greece or Rome—society operated on the basis of radically different values. Consider in particular the emphasis on humility in today's society, in comparison with, say, what we find in the work of the ancient Greek philosopher Aristotle,* whose ideal was the "great-souled man" who took pride in acknowledging his own greatness. In the post-Enlightenment Western world, many of us are still guided by a moral code inherited from Judeo-Christian religious traditions, while at the same time leading secular, or even atheist, lives. Nietzsche urges us to take a less passive approach to our moral views.

What Nietzsche achieves in *Genealogy*, then, is to open up a psychological space of self-exploration, in which we can closely question the values we have inherited. By charting the historical origins of our moral values we will thus see that they are not absolute, but merely contingent developments: products of circumstance and highly complex historical events.

Once we have understood the roots of our current moral ideals, we will be far better positioned to inquire as to what relevance they now hold for us.

Nietzsche's *Genealogy* is a fine example of his stylistic prowess, and even when translated into English retains a power and elegance that far surpasses almost everything that has been written on moral philosophy since. The text also contains a wealth of detail, juxtaposing classical scholarship and history together with empirical* speculation and insights into subjects as diverse as economic history and developmental biology. Nietzsche was able to combine the strengths of both the Enlightenment tradition of rational, scientific investigation and the values of sensitive, learned inquiry into history and culture founded on the principles of Romanticism* (a European intellectual and cultural movement, arising as a reaction to the Enlightenment, that emphasized emotion, creativity, imagination, and individuality).

Above all, the text is highly enjoyable: rather than focusing on dry, technical arguments, Nietzsche appeals to our emotions, and with fiery prose designed to be highly persuasive takes the reader on a journey of self-exploration that will ultimately enable us to better understand our deepest moral and personal commitments.

NOTES

1   Rüdiger Safranski, *Nietzsche: A Philosophical Biography*, trans. Shelley Frisch (London, Granta Books, 2002), 45.

2   Friedrich Nietzsche, *On the Genealogy of Morality*, trans. Maudemarie Clark and Alan Swensen (Indianapolis: Hackett Publishing Co., 1998), introduction, xi.

SECTION 1
INFLUENCES

MODULE 1
THE AUTHOR AND THE
HISTORICAL CONTEXT

KEY POINTS

- In *On the Genealogy of Morality*, Nietzsche launches a strong and sustained challenge to many of our most deeply held values.

- Nietzsche came from a religious family of Protestant* ministers; he studied theology and philology* at the University of Bonn.

- He reacted negatively against many of the dominant social and intellectual trends of his time—especially the growing nationalism of his native Prussia* (a European state that had by this time become part of a unified Germany).

Why Read This Text?

On the Genealogy of Morality (1887) marks the highpoint of Nietzsche's continuing campaign against the Judeo-Christian* morality characterized by the ideals of compassion, selflessness, piety, and chastity which was dominant in his contemporary Europe. Nietzsche sought to challenge its influence, stating that "*for once the value of these values must itself be called into question.*"[1] He later argued that this morality may have been serving to inhibit the spiritual growth of humanity.

Nietzsche is therefore questioning the foundations of some of our core beliefs, and asking us to find "new interpretations and meanings for our ethical practices."[2] He also aims to show us that there are many other possible forms of ethical life—for example, the noble morality characterized by an admiration for bravery, strength, honor, and

> ❝ Given a skepticism that is characteristic of me, to which I reluctantly admit—for it is directed towards *morality*, towards everything on earth that has until now been celebrated as morality—a skepticism that first appeared so early in my life, so spontaneously, so irrepressibly, so much in contradiction to my environment, age, models, origins, that I almost have the right to call it my '*a priori*'—it was inevitable that early on my curiosity and my suspicion as well would stop at the question: *what*, in fact, is the *origin* of our good and evil? ❞
>
> Friedrich Nietzsche, *On the Genealogy of Morality*

success in battle that he associates with the heroes of ancient Greece and Rome—so that we no longer take the Christian interpretation of morality for granted.

Author's Life

Nietzsche was born in the small village of Röcken in Prussian Saxony, in October 1844. His father Carl had been the town minister, his uncle and both grandfathers were ministers, and his paternal grandfather was also a noted scholar in the Protestant* tradition (together with Catholicism and the Eastern Orthodox Church, one of the three principal branches of the Christian faith). After the death of his father in 1849 and his brother Joseph the year after, Nietzsche was raised in the "feminine and pious"[3] society of his mother, his sister, a grandmother, and two aunts. Between the ages of 14 and 19, Nietzsche attended Schulpforta, a famous boarding school that had formerly been a monastery. Yet when Nietzsche went to study theology and philology at the University of Bonn in 1864, he quickly lost interest in theology and moved with his "favorite teacher"[4] Friedrich Ritschl* to continue studying philology at the University of Leipzig in 1865. Partly in reaction to his oppressive Lutheran*upbringing, Nietzsche later produced a series of devastating attacks on organized religion.

After serving his compulsory military service for a year, he was appointed, at the age of just 24 and on Ritschl's recommendation, as associate professor of philology at the University of Basel in 1869. Ritschl, a leading classical scholar, was very impressed with the young Nietzsche, announcing that he had "never had such a talented student."[5] Nietzsche withdrew from academic life in 1879, partly for health reasons and partly from disappointment with scholarly life. He spent the next decade living a solitary, nomadic existence traveling around France, Germany, Switzerland, and Italy, until suffering a complete and permanent mental breakdown in January 1889.

Author's Background

Nietzsche was writing at a time of increased cultural, political, and intellectual confidence in his native German state of Prussia. The Prussian state was now part of a unified German Empire that had been founded in 1871 under a constitution designed four years earlier by its first chancellor, Otto von Bismarck,* the former Prussian prime minister and the dominant political force of the period.

Though Nietzsche's frequently anti-democratic views in *Genealogy* seem to resonate with Bismarck's mantra that "blood and iron" rather than majority persuasion is of first importance in politics, Nietzsche was nevertheless "increasingly appalled by the political atmosphere (especially the nationalism and anti-Semitism)" in Germany, and wrote most of his works in "voluntary exile"[6] after leaving the University of Basel. This attitude finds expression in the anti-nationalist sentiment of the text, where he writes of the "deep, icy mistrust that the German stirs up as soon as he comes into power."[7]

Nietzsche was also interested in the arts, but in contrast to popular belief at the time, he saw contemporary German culture as degenerate, empty, unoriginal, and lacking a "unity of artistic style."[8] Throughout his career and in *Genealogy* in particular, he often plays the role of cultural critic, seeking to provoke a rejuvenation of German culture.

NOTES

1   Friedrich Nietzsche, *On the Genealogy of Morality*, trans. Maudemarie Clark and Alan Swensen (Indianapolis: Hackett Publishing Co., 1998), 5.

2   Nietzsche, *Genealogy*, 16.

3   Friedrich Copleston, *A History of Philosophy*, vol. 7, *Eighteenth- and Nineteenth-Century German Philosophy* (London: Bloomsbury, 2013), 390.

4   Walter Kaufmann, *Nietzsche: Philosopher, Psychologist, Antichrist* (New Jersey: Princeton University Press, 1974), 24.

5   Rüdiger Safranski, *Nietzsche: A Philosophical Biography*, trans. Shelley Frisch (London, Granta Books, 2002), 45.

6   Nietzsche, *Genealogy*, 9.

7   Nietzsche, *Genealogy*, 23.

8   Friedrich Nietzsche, *Untimely Meditations*, trans. R. J. Hollingdale, ed. Daniel Breazeale (Cambridge: Cambridge University Press, 1997), 5.

MODULE 2
ACADEMIC CONTEXT

KEY POINTS

- A dominant concern of moral philosophers since the period of European intellectual history known as the Enlightenment* has been to provide a rational basis for morality.

- Contemporary thinkers, influenced by the English naturalist Charles Darwin,* the chief proponent of the theory of evolution by natural selection, had enquired into morality's historical origins instead.

- Nietzsche rejected their approaches and instead aimed to pursue the question from the point of view of psychology and cultural history rather than evolutionary biology alone.

The Work in its Context

Friedrich Nietzsche wrote *On the Genealogy of Morality* during a time when the landscape of moral philosophy was changing. Between roughly 1630 and 1850, moral philosophers had been concerned with the Enlightenment project of providing a comprehensive moral philosophy together with a secular, rational justification for it. Thinkers who had contributed to this project were diverse and include the philosophers Immanuel Kant,* Denis Diderot,* David Hume,* and John Stuart Mill,* and the eighteenth-century Scottish economist and social theorist Adam Smith.*[1] Yet the conclusions of these moral philosophers were highly similar: as Nietzsche often pointed out, each had inherited their values "from their shared Christian past."[2]

The defining intellectual achievement of the era was Charles Darwin's work *On the Origin of Species*, published in 1859. The doctrine of evolution—that species are not immutable but rather change over

> ❝ Philosophers, Nietzsche claims, have conceived their task and themselves as if they were simply rational subjects, have tended to devalue their own feelings and subjectivity, the body, and even the entire empirical world of change, imperfection, and transience, and have sought something 'higher', more 'real' or 'objective,' in subservience to which they must suppress their natural selves. ❞
>
> Christopher Janaway, *Beyond Selflessness*

time—was not itself new and had been explored by others such as the English philosopher Herbert Spencer*. Darwin added to this two further ideas. First, he argued that life descends from a single common source through a branching pattern. Second, he convincingly showed that the primary mechanism driving this process is natural selection*— where members of a species more suited to their environments are better able to survive and reproduce, passing on favorable characteristics to their offspring. This negates the need for purposeful progress toward a specific, inevitable goal. In *The Descent of Man* and *The Expression of the Emotions in Man and Animals,* Darwin applies his approach to human psychology, opening the door for a new kind of moral inquiry whereby rather than giving abstract rational justifications for their assertions, philosophers would show morality to be a natural outcome of the forces of natural selection.

Overview of the Field

The typical approach philosophers had taken in justifying their shared Christian morality was to base it on a key proposition that would "characterize some feature or features of human nature."[3] For instance, the German philosopher Immanuel Kant aimed to base morality on the rules that any human being was obliged to follow simply by virtue

21

of his or her rational capacities, "to give to him, as a rational being, laws *a priori*."[4] On the other hand, the skeptical Scottish thinker David Hume and the French Enlightenment philosopher Denis Diderot began from what they took to be universal human desires and inclinations, and built their systems from here.

It was clear to Nietzsche that these Enlightenment projects had failed; in his previous book, *Beyond Good and Evil,* he describes Kant's reasoning as "tartuffery" (implying that all the rigmarole of his ethical theory is just for show) and Benedict Spinoza's* as "hocus pocus," and indeed they are not explicitly mentioned in *Genealogy* though they provide the background to the debate.[5]

Nietzsche does respond directly to some other thinkers that also attempt to account for the origins of morality naturalistically: that is, in terms of natural forces alone. He provides short discussions of the work of the philosophers Paul Rée* and Herbert Spencer, which would apply equally well to the English philosopher John Stuart Mill and to David Hume. Yet for Nietzsche these philosophers had all made several crucial mistakes.

First, their earlier accounts had invariably remained purely hypothetical and ahistorical, with insufficient attention to concrete, documentable fact.

Second, these "English psychologists"* (a pejorative term Nietzsche uses for this group of thinkers who aimed to account for morality in purely evolutionary terms) had falsely assumed that their own particular way of looking at morality, which was largely centered on selflessness, was universal and shared by all peoples in all periods of history. For Nietzsche, the assumed equivalence of "good" and "unegoistic" is founded on a prejudice.

Third, they tried to show that morality had developed because it was useful, and so ultimately helped humans to survive and reproduce more effectively. This fitted well with the then-dominant utilitarianism: an approach to moral philosophy advocated by Mill and Bentham, according to which we should always do the action which maximises the general well-being of society as understood in terms of pleasure and pain. In contrast, for Nietzsche, morality primarily concerns the acknowledgment of distinctions of spiritual rank.

Academic Influences

Crucial to an understanding of Nietzsche's thought is the atheist philosopher Arthur Schopenhauer:* "[T]he issue for me," Nietzsche wrote, "was the *value* of morality—and over this I had to struggle almost solely with my great teacher Schopenhauer."[6] Nietzsche was initially influenced by Schopenhauer's explanation of motivation in terms of pleasure and pain, although he later came to regard this as too simplistic. Schopenhauer's conviction that selfless thought and action lie at the heart of moral behavior comes under explicit criticism in *Genealogy*.

Nietzsche was also influenced by the German philosopher Friedrich Lange's* 1865 book *The History of Materialism* and *Criticism of its Present Importance*, which offers a critical discussion of attempts to explain the whole of reality in purely mechanical terms.[7] In the late 1860s Nietzsche wrote: "Kant, Schopenhauer and this book by Lange—I do not need anything else,"[8] evidence of how pivotal Lange's discussion of scientific approaches to philosophical questions was on Nietzsche's thought. Although he eventually moved away from the view of science as the highest human achievement, as exemplified in *Human, All Too Human* (1880), Nietzsche always retained a belief in the value of scientific techniques, and this is reflected in his approach in *Genealogy*.

Other important influences included Ralph Waldo Emerson,* the American essayist who brought about "Nietzsche's very first important encounter with philosophy" and was perhaps his "most read and reread author";[9] the Greek philosopher Plato, whom Nietzsche "refers to more frequently than any other with the exception of Schopenhauer,"[10] and whom he saw as his "true great opponent";[11] the acclaimed Russian novelist Fyodor Dostoevsky,* "the only psychologist who had anything to teach me";[12] the French moralists, such as François de La Rochefoucauld,* who influenced Nietzsche's often pithy, aphoristic style; and the many other ancient Greek philosophers he encountered in his training as a classical philologist.

NOTES

1   Alasdair MacIntyre, *After Virtue: A Study in Moral Theory* (London: Bloomsbury, 2011), 62.

2   MacIntyre, *After Virtue*, 62.

3   MacIntyre, *After Virtue*, 62.

4   Immanuel Kant, *Practical Philosophy*, trans. Mary Gregor (Cambridge: Cambridge University Press, 1996), 45.

5   MacIntyre, *After Virtue*, 46–7.

6   Friedrich Nietzsche, *On the Genealogy of Morality*, trans. Maudemarie Clark and Alan Swensen (Indianapolis: Hackett Publishing Co., 1998), 4.

7   Friedrich Albert Lange, *The History of Materialism and Criticism of its Present Importance*, trans. Ernest Chester Thomas (Humanities Press, 1950).

8   Thomas Brobjer, *Nietzsche's Philosophical Context: An Intellectual Biography* (Chicago: University of Illinois Press, 2008), 35.

9   Brobjer, *Nietzsche's Philosophical Context*, 22, 23.

10 Brobjer, *Nietzsche's Philosophical Context*, 25.

11 Brobjer, *Nietzsche's Philosophical Context*, 28.

12 Friedrich Nietzsche, *The Anti-Christ, Ecce Homo, Twilight of the Idols. And Other Writings*, trans. Judith Norman, ed. Aaron Ridley (Cambridge: Cambridge University Press, 2005), 219.

MODULE 3
THE PROBLEM

KEY POINTS

- The key problem for Nietzsche and his contemporaries was to account for the origins of their inherited morality.
- At the time, the dominant approach tried to explain morality by looking at its current usefulness for society.
- For Nietzsche, historical inquiry reveals that the valuation "good" emerged as a mark of distinction of rank rather than denoting what was useful for society as a whole.

Core Question

In writing *On the Genealogy of Morality* in 1887, Friedrich Nietzsche was contributing to a philosophical tradition that harked back to the work of the Scottish philosopher David Hume.* He aimed to locate the origin of our moral values in the natural world, "in terms of human psychology and without resorting to God or metaphysics."[1] Since Hume, two important events had occurred: the rapid growth of evolutionary biology spurred by the publication of Charles Darwin's* influential book of evolutionary theory *On the Origin of Species* in 1859, and the articulation and development of utilitarian* ethics by Jeremy Bentham* and then John Stuart Mill* (according to which the moral worth of an action is determined by its overall impact on the total happiness of all members of society).

In *On Natural Selection,* Darwin describes nature as a harsh competition for resources, in which only a fortunate elite are able to thrive. At the same time, there are variations across individuals of a given species, some of which enable their offspring to enjoy a higher chance of surviving and reproducing. Because many of these variations

> 66 The project of a genealogy of morality is thus to explain in purely naturalistic terms, without appeal to the voice of God or an immortal soul in touch with eternal values, the origins of morality: how it came about that human beings are guided by morality. The question is not why we are morally good, but why it is that human animals accept (hence act on the basis of) specifically *moral* reasons or values. 99
>
> Maudemarie Clarke, introduction to *On the Genealogy of Morality*

can be passed from one generation to the next, over time favorable variations are passed on and accentuated.

The utilitarian ethics of Bentham and Mill located the moral worth of an action in its practical consequences; specifically in how much pleasure it would bring to those affected. According to Bentham, "it is the greatest happiness of the greatest number that is the measure of right and wrong."[2] With this idea in common currency, an obvious strategy for would-be "genealogists" of morality emerged: if our current moral beliefs and practices do have socially beneficial consequences, morality might thereby be explained as a product of natural selection.

The Participants

There were many thinkers who attempted to give a Darwinian account of morality, including Darwin himself. Particularly salient for Nietzsche was a group of loosely connected thinkers he calls the "English psychologists."[*3] He mentions Paul Rée* and Herbert Spencer* by name, though the term would also apply to others such as John Stuart Mill and the Scottish thinker David Hume.

Rée argues in his book *On the Origins of Moral Sensations* (1887) that over many generations in human prehistory we developed altruistic (selfless) drives due to the inherent usefulness of those drives for human society and the pressures of natural selection: hence "moral phenomena can be traced back to natural causes just as much as physical phenomena."[4] Later in the development of a society, the connection to utility is forgotten and selfless actions are simply pursued "as if they were good in themselves."[5]

The philosopher Herbert Spencer argued for the utilitarian view that good actions are simply those actions that have useful consequences, and that these are therefore reinforced over time for this very reason. Hume's account is similar; he writes that "the benevolent or softer affections are Estimable; and, wherever they appear, engage the approbation, and good will of mankind."[6] These accounts differ from Rée's in that the useful consequences of morality are continually affirmed rather than being forgotten over time.

The Contemporary Debate

Nietzsche attacks Rée's view directly in the text, writing of his "clear, tidy and smart, even overly smart little book" that "I may have never read anything to which I so emphatically said 'no'."[7] Perhaps most problematic for Nietzsche is the "inherent psychological absurdity" of society coming to forget the usefulness of selfless actions, even though "this usefulness has been the everyday experience in all ages" and is "continually underscored anew."[8] Nietzsche regarded Spencer's (and implicitly Hume's) view as "much more reasonable"[9] and "psychologically tenable," though he still argued that this "path of explanation is also false."[10]

What both thinkers had wrong, according to Nietzsche, was that the term "good" was in fact not coined by the recipients of the good action, "those to whom 'goodness' is rendered."[11] Rather, it was the "noble, powerful, higher-ranking and high-minded"[12] individuals who first applied the term to themselves, in order to be distinguished and separated from "everything base, low-minded, common, and vulgar."[13] At first the term was therefore simply a mark of status, and only later did it take on a morally charged interpretation.

NOTES

1   Friedrich Nietzsche, *On the Genealogy of Morality*, trans. Maudemarie Clark and Alan Swensen (Indianapolis: Hackett Publishing Co., 1998), introduction, xxiii.

2   Jeremy Bentham, *A Fragment on Government* (New Jersey: The Lawbook Exchange, 2001), 93.

3   Nietzsche, *Genealogy*, 9.

4   Paul Rée, *Basic Writings*, trans. and ed. Robin Small (Urbana: University of Illinois Press, 2003), 87.

5   Nietzsche, *Genealogy*, 10.

6   David Hume, *An Enquiry Concerning the Principles of Morals* (Indianapolis: Hackett Publishing Co., 1983), 16–17.

7   Nietzsche, *Genealogy*, 3.

8   Nietzsche, *Genealogy*, 11.

9   Nietzsche, *Genealogy*, 11.

10 Nietzsche, *Genealogy*, 12.

11 Nietzsche, *Genealogy*, 10.

12 Nietzsche, *Genealogy*, 10.

13 Nietzsche, *Genealogy*, 10.

MODULE 4
THE AUTHOR'S CONTRIBUTION

KEY POINTS

- Nietzsche argues that rather than being universal, inevitable, and absolute, our contemporary moral ideals have arisen through highly particular historical developments and may now be undermining mankind's true development.

- Nietzsche brought a fresh historical spirit to the inquiry, changing the standards pertaining to accounts of morality's origins.

- His sharply critical line was highly original and the product of a unique thinker concerned with distancing himself from his contemporaries.

Author's Aims

Friedrich Nietzsche's 1887 work *On the Genealogy of Morality* aims to give a naturalistic* account of the origins of Judeo-Christian* morality—that is, one that appeals only to natural forms of explanation, rather than to metaphysical or divine causes. He pursues this project across three historical essays, each describing the development of a different aspect of moral life. The first examines our notions of "good" and "evil"—which, for Nietzsche, apply primarily to people rather than to individual actions. The second looks at our moral conscience, and concepts of responsibility and punishment. The third inquires into our current views about the point and purpose of human life as a whole, which Nietzsche sums up in the phrase the "ascetic ideal"— the pious life of charity, abstinence, selflessness and compassion for others.

Instead of starting from the moral assumptions of his European

> ❝ Nietzsche's difference from other naturalistic philosophers must be sought first in his profound concern whether universally valid values and a meaningful life are at all possible in a godless world, and secondly in his impassioned scorn for those who simply take for granted the validity of any particular set of values which happens to have the sanction of their religion, class, society, or state. He did not consider it the philosopher's task to develop his ingenuity, or his disingenuousness, in 'the finding of bad reasons for what we believe on instinct.' ❞
>
> Walter Kaufmann, *Nietzsche: Philosopher, Psychologist, Antichrist*

contemporaries, Nietzsche followed a more historical approach that opened up new lines of thought that had been unavailable to them. Though not quite supplying enough concrete evidence to fulfill his ambition of grounding his narrative in "that which can be really documented,"[1] and often remaining vague about details of the events he describes, Nietzsche convincingly shows that there have been societies that employed moral frameworks entirely different from our own. Consequently, our own moral standpoint must be measured against these rival possibilities for ethical life.

Approach

Nietzsche regarded himself as the first thinker to attempt a truly historical analysis of the origins of morality, writing of his contemporaries and predecessors that "it is certain that they lack the historical spirit itself."[2] In place of accurate history grounded in fact, these thinkers had, in Nietzsche's view, substituted mere "hypothesizing into the blue"[3]—simply finding a "single contemporary purpose or meaning in some human institution" and assuming that this was "the cause of the institution's coming into being."[4] In contrast, Nietzsche uses his vast knowledge of linguistic and cultural history to put contemporary morality into context, referring to peoples as diverse as the Celts and the Chinese.[5]

Another way in which Nietzsche's approach was unique is that his history of our inherited morality was only intended as a preliminary task for "something much more important"[6]—an inquiry into the value of this morality, especially in comparison with other ways of thinking and feeling. Nietzsche hoped that he would inspire future philosophers to take up an honest inquiry into the actual value of moral precepts for human life today, and not simply justify them through rational argumentation. He saw philosophers as being entrusted with the tasks of providing new ideals to strive toward, of legislating new moral precepts to live by, and of introducing alternative, more life-enhancing moral sentiments.

Contribution in Context

Among the European moral theorists of the eighteenth and nineteenth centuries, Nietzsche's work clearly stands apart from the rest. In attempting to account for moral phenomena in non-moral, scientific terms, Nietzsche had a number of predecessors. They were, however, never equipped with the right tools to tackle the problem, lacking the deep historical knowledge, strong psychological instincts, and thorough understanding of language that Nietzsche was able to supply. Even the philosopher David Hume,* famous in his time for writing a learned history of England, failed to account for the diversity of moral viewpoints and their historically situated character.[7]

In contrast, Nietzsche aimed to write a narrative that was detailed, accurate, and highly original. As a thinker who held that nothing should be taken for granted and everything is open to critique, he would rarely pick up an idea or argument and employ it in his own work without modification. Even Darwin's theory of evolution by natural selection comes under criticism as making too little of the forces of individual self-assertion common to all life. Often writing in isolation, Nietzsche possessed both deep cultural and historical knowledge and profound classical scholarship, as well as uncanny psychological instincts. This enabled him to take a far subtler and more comprehensive approach than his predecessors.

NOTES

1   Friedrich Nietzsche, *On the Genealogy of Morality*, trans. Maudemarie Clark and Alan Swensen (Indianapolis: Hackett Publishing Co., 1998), 6.

2   Nietzsche, *Genealogy*, 10.

3   Nietzsche, *Genealogy*, 6.

4   Christopher Janaway, *Beyond Selflessness: Reading Nietzsche's* Genealogy (Oxford: Oxford University Press, 2007), 50.

5   Nietzsche, *Genealogy*, 53.

6   Nietzsche, *Genealogy*, 4.

7   Nietzsche, *Genealogy*, introduction, xxiii.

SECTION 2
IDEAS

MODULE 5
MAIN IDEAS

KEY POINTS

- Nietzsche's central themes in *Genealogy* are the distinction between "master" and "slave" moralities, our moral conscience as a repression and redirection of instincts to cruelty, and the ascetic ideal as a conception of life's highest purpose.

- Through discussing the historical development of these phenomena, Nietzsche argues that our current moral valuations may prevent the development of the most noble and spiritually healthy kinds of people.

- These three themes are approached through three powerfully wrought essays, in which Nietzsche shows off his stylistic and rhetorical prowess.

Key Themes

In the first essay of *On the Genealogy of Morality*, "'Good and Evil,' 'Good and Bad,'" Friedrich Nietzsche compares different moralities, observing that they fall into two types. There are "noble moralities," according to which we see strong individuals with a "powerful physicality"[1] and "blossoming, rich, even overflowing health"[2] designate themselves as "good" in opposition to those they consider "bad" (meaning base or unworthy). And there are also "slave moralities," which are the prerogative of weak individuals who must band together as a herd for safety. Under this latter system of values, the noble class—seen through the "poisonous eye of *ressentiment*"*[3] (a term of art for Nietzsche, denoting repressed anger at one's station in life)—are designated "evil," and the slaves then label themselves "good" only reactively. These two forms of valuation and their interaction

> " Of all that has been done on earth against 'the
> noble,' 'the mighty,' 'the lords,' 'the power-holders,'
> nothing is worthy of mention in comparison with that
> which the *Jews* have done against them: the Jews, that
> priestly people who in the end were only able to obtain
> satisfaction from their enemies and conquerors through
> a radical revaluation of their values, that is, through an
> act of *spiritual revenge.* "
>
> Friedrich Nietzsche, *On the Genealogy of Morality*

constitute the first essay's central topic.

In the second essay, "'Guilt,' 'Bad Conscience,' and Related Matters," Nietzsche explains how the human moral conscience has developed in history and prehistory. Beginning from a picture of human life characterized by primitive creditor–debtor relationships, he explains how we have arrived at our current ways of thinking. The most important idea here is *sublimation*,* which describes how through historical processes human instincts can be reoriented and redirected to other, often more civilized purposes. In his earlier work *Human, All Too Human,* Nietzsche had already suggested that the traits humans had taken as an expression of a higher nature—including the moral conscience—could, in fact, be understood as reinterpretations of lower, baser traits. While many thinkers see the moral conscience as a mark of our divine origins, which shows us to be wholly separate and different in kind from other animals, Nietzsche instead positions it as an outcome of our civilization's barbaric history.

The third essay, "What do Ascetic Ideals Mean?," discusses the conception of the good life as the monkish life of prayer, "poverty, humility, chastity,"[4] and self-denial: the "anti-sensual metaphysics of priests."[5] Though he labels the ideal as life-denying, claiming that it "treats life as a wrong path that one must finally retrace,"[6] Nietzsche regards this as the only viable ideal humanity has produced so far.

Exploring the Ideas

In addition to the noble and inferior classes described above, Nietzsche also introduces another group in his first essay: the priests. These individuals stir up the *ressentiment**of the slave class and ultimately enable them to achieve a kind of "spiritual revenge"[7] for their subjugation with a "slave revolt in morality."[8] That is, over time they universalize their own moral code, one that reveres humbleness and passivity. However, while suitable for a mediocre type of person, the slave morality is unhealthy for the spiritually superior, stunting their ability to reach their full potential with restrictive ideas of what it means to be "good." According to Nietzsche, there is a danger that slave morality might be "to blame if the *highest power and splendour* of the human type—in itself possible—were never attained."[9]

In the second essay, Nietzsche argues that an understanding of guilt and moral conscience must begin with primitive creditor–debtor relationships, "the oldest and most primitive relationship among persons."[10] "In *this* sphere, in contract law that is," he writes, "the moral conceptual world 'guilt,' 'conscience,' 'duty,' 'sacredness of duty' has its genesis."[11] When a debtor failed to pay what he owed, a creditor would inflict physical injury as punishment, enabling them to feel powerful and so providing a "*feeling of satisfaction* as repayment."[12] As civilization progresses, these barbaric practices are gradually prohibited. Nietzsche, however, proposes that our instincts themselves do not then simply disappear as humankind becomes more civilized: rather, they merely "*turn themselves inwards*"[13] against ourselves: "*that* is the origin of 'bad conscience.'"[14]

Nietzsche's discussion of the "ascetic ideal" in the third essay portrays it as a culturally dominant conception of the ultimate "point and value of human life."[15] Individuals try to find meaning in life through following the ascetic ideal, but ultimately end up turning away from it entirely. However, Nietzsche sees the ascetic ideal as the only option for trying to lead a meaningful life that humankind has put forward. The modern scientific drive toward absolute truth at all costs—often taken to oppose the religious mind-set and provide an alternative set of values—is seen as merely a development of the virtue of truthfulness: "It is still a *metaphysical* belief on which our belief in science rests."[16]

Language and Expression

Nietzsche's style is often highly rhetorical—that is, rather than convincing his readers solely with logic, he aims to rouse strong emotions and to disrupt our established patterns of thought through the use of persuasive language. In the analytic* philosophical tradition associated with Anglo-American inquiry, this unconventional prose style served to delay his recognition as a serious philosopher; indeed, his frequently hostile and cynical tone was for a long time "enough to keep the majority of its practitioners from even reading him" according to the Nietzsche scholar Maudemarie Clark.*[17]

To express his novel ideas, Nietzsche sometimes coins new terms such as *ressentiment** in order to make his meaning clear. Nietzsche also frequently uses phrases drawn from other languages rather than his native German to convey the subtle nuances necessary to express his views, including the Latin *toto caelo* ("as far apart as possible"),[18] the French *partie honteuse* ("shameful part"),[19] the Sanskrit *arya* ("noble"),[20] and the ancient Greek *kakos* (meaning bad or worthless).[21]

The three themes discussed across the three essays should not be seen as cleanly separable; cross-references occur throughout, and in the third essay earlier themes are revisited in depth. Put together, the three essays present a unified picture of our current morality, together with a searing critique of this outlook and suggestions of ways in which it might now be holding back our spiritual development.

NOTES

1   Friedrich Nietzsche, *On the Genealogy of Morality*, trans. Maudemarie Clark and Alan Swensen (Indianapolis: Hackett Publishing Co., 1998), 16.

2   Nietzsche, *Genealogy*, 16.

3   Nietzsche, *Genealogy*, 22.

4   Nietzsche, *Genealogy*, 76.

5   Nietzsche, *Genealogy*, 15.

6   Nietzsche, *Genealogy*, 83.

7   Nietzsche, *Genealogy*, introduction, xxx.

8   Nietzsche, *Genealogy*, 19.

9   Nietzsche, *Genealogy*, 5.

10 Nietzsche, *Genealogy*, 45.

11 Nietzsche, *Genealogy*, 41.

12 Nietzsche, *Genealogy*, 41.

13 Nietzsche, *Genealogy*, 57.

14 Nietzsche, *Genealogy*, 57.

15 Nietzsche, *Genealogy*, introduction, xxvi.

16 Nietzsche, *Genealogy*, 110.

17 Nietzsche, *Genealogy*, introduction, xiii.

18 "By a tremendous distance." Nietzsche, *Genealogy*, 3.

19 "Shameful part." Nietzsche, *Genealogy*, 9.

20 "Noble." Nietzsche, *Genealogy*, 13.

21 "Bad, ugly, ill-born, base, cowardly, ignoble." Nietzsche, *Genealogy*, 13.

MODULE 6
SECONDARY IDEAS

KEY POINTS

- Nietzsche also discusses the historical origins of our social practices—such as our institutions of punishment—and the central role of unconscious drives and desires.

- His views on these themes influenced many later thinkers in the humanities and in psychology.

- Perhaps most influential was his view of human beings as largely motivated by unconscious and irrational desires, an idea that would influence generations of psychologists from Sigmund Freud* onward.

Other Ideas

Throughout *On the Genealogy of Morality*, Friedrich Nietzsche often stresses the inadequacy of utilitarian* explanations of social developments such as our institutions of punishment. He was critical of a group of thinkers he called the "English psychologists,"* who tried to explain them with reference to their usefulness. Nietzsche explains how they would first find a purpose for these practices, and then "innocently place this purpose at the beginning"[1] as the underlying cause. In contrast to this "naïve" and simplistic approach, Nietzsche argues that the ultimate explanation for punishment is not rational, but emotive: punishment stems "from anger over an injury suffered, which is vented on the agent of the injury."[2]

Like many contemporary philosophers, Nietzsche is interested in shedding light on the meaning of moral concepts. As a philologist* he naturally approaches this task through historical and linguistic inquiry, and the starting point for his inquiry was the question, "What do the

> ❝ The 'development' of a thing, a practice, an organ is accordingly least of all its *progressus* toward a goal, still less a logical and shortest *progressus*, reached with the smallest expenditure of energy and cost—but rather the succession of more or less profound, more or less independent processes of overpowering that play themselves out in it. ❞
>
> Friedrich Nietzsche, *On the Genealogy of Morality*

terms coined for 'good' in the various languages actually mean from an etymological* viewpoint?"[3] At the end of the first essay he suggests the following title for an academic essay contest: "What clues does the study of language, in particular etymological research, provide for the history of the development of moral concepts?"[4] Nietzsche goes some way to answering the question in the text—for example, using arguments based on linguistic analysis to show that "good" was initially associated with nobility, and "bad" with those who were base or inferior.

For Nietzsche, the greater part of human thought and action is motivated by unconscious desires and primitive, sometimes barbaric instincts. In his earlier work *Human, All Too Human* (1878), Nietzsche argued for an idea stressed by Darwin: that the traits humanity had most prized as proof of their superiority could be explained as developments of "traits and activities that are easily recognized as 'lower,' as continuous with those of other animals."[5] By the time he wrote *Genealogy*, even philosophical thinking itself is seen as based on unconscious motivations: "every animal, thus also *la bête philosophe* [the philosophical animal], instinctively strives for an optimum of favourable conditions under which it can vent its power completely."[6]

Exploring the Ideas

Utilitarians since Jeremy Bentham,*—the founder of the school—
had asserted that the purpose of punishment lies in its usefulness for
society. Nietzsche argued, however, that the so-called "purposes" of
punishment are merely changing, "after the fact"[7] interpretations of a
core practice; understanding these purposes does not imply that we
have "comprehended anything regarding its genesis."[8] Nietzsche then
lists many different interpretations that have existed over time, such as
"Punishment as rendering-harmless," "Punishment as instilling fear of
those who determine and execute the punishment," and "Punishment
as a kind of compensation," to name just three.[9]

In *Philosophical Investigations* (1953), the Austrian philosopher
Ludwig Wittgenstein*—who had read Nietzsche—likened the
meaning of a word to a length of rope that is constructed out of many
loose fibers, illustrating the variety of words' overlapping uses.[10] This
image captures Nietzsche's emphasis on the multiple intersecting
processes and forces that give meaning to any word or concept (such
as "punishment") that has a complicated history. The strands can only
be unraveled by looking at the development of the concept from
earlier stages, before the various uses and purposes have been woven
together to form a "unity that is difficult to dissolve."[11]

Another theme Nietzsche continues to return to is that prior to
man "finding himself enclosed once and for all within the sway of
society and peace"[12] in the modern age, our behavior was once much
less constrained and more natural. It is only with the new set of
challenges introduced by civilization that we are so often reduced to
explicit rational thinking, to relying on our "poorest and most erring
organ."[13]

Overlooked

Nietzsche's insistent call for philosophers to pay careful attention to
the actual history of words has largely been ignored by contemporary

Anglophone moral philosophy. Philosophers working today continue to analyze our moral concepts in a largely ahistorical way, using only logic and introspection—with some notable exceptions, such as the twentieth-century British philosophers Alasdair MacIntyre* and Bernard Williams.* This may be because philosophers tend to lack sufficient scholarly training—a deficiency Nietzsche himself was fond of pointing out, writing that a lack of historical sense was the "hereditary defect"[14] of philosophers.

Another overlooked idea concerns philosophical investigation of the habits of thought formed by the grammatical structure of languages. For instance, Nietzsche claims that belief in a metaphysical "subject"— a determinate and essentially unified self— is merely a "seduction of language,"[15] referring here to "subject" in the grammatical sense, to which verbs and adjectives are attached in sentences, such as the French philosopher René Descartes' pronouncement: "I am thinking." Elsewhere, Nietzsche writes that "I fear we do not get rid of God, because we still believe in grammar."[16]

Although connections between metaphysical views and the surface grammatical structure of language has often been at center-stage in contemporary moral philosophy and metaphysics, Nietzsche's early contribution to this approach and the psychological and historical techniques he introduced are often overlooked.

NOTES

1   Friedrich Nietzsche, *On the Genealogy of Morality*, trans. Clark and Alan Swensen (Indianapolis: Hackett Publishing Co., 1998), 50.

2   Nietzsche, *Genealogy*, 39.

3   Nietzsche, *Genealogy*, 12.

4   Nietzsche, *Genealogy*, 33.

5   Nietzsche, *Genealogy*, xxii.

6   Nietzsche, *Genealogy*, 75.

7   Nietzsche, *Genealogy*, 53.

8   Nietzsche, *Genealogy*, 51.

9   Nietzsche, *Genealogy*, 53.

10 Ludwig Wittgenstein, *The Blue and Brown Books* (Oxford: Blackwell, 1958), 87.

11 Nietzsche, *Genealogy*, 53.

12 Nietzsche, *Genealogy*, 56.

13 Nietzsche, *Genealogy*, 54.

14 Bernard Williams, *Truth and Truthfulness: An Essay in Genealogy* (Princeton: Princeton University Press, 2002).

15 Nietzsche, *Genealogy*, 25.

16 Friedrich Nietzsche, *The Anti-Christ, Ecce Homo, Twilight of the Idols. And Other Writings*, trans. Judith Norman, ed. Aaron Ridley (Cambridge: Cambridge University Press, 2005), 17.

MODULE 7
ACHIEVEMENT

KEY POINTS

- Although never quite producing the factual and concretely documented historical analysis his introductory remarks promise, Nietzsche did achieve his goal of writing a powerful and psychologically effective critique of contemporary morality.

- The insight and erudition Nietzsche was able to exhibit in *Genealogy* was the result of his intensive classical training, which enabled him to approach the problems from a new direction to that of other naturalistic philosophers such as the "English psychologists."*

- Nietzsche's personal relationships were rather meager, as he spent much of his life in isolation from intellectual and social contact. This has led to some of his views seeming insular or even extreme.

Assessing the Argument

Friedrich Nietzsche intended the critical history of contemporary European morality that unfolds in his *On the Genealogy of Morality* to be grounded in concrete and documentable historical fact, whereas those written by his contemporaries such as Paul Rée,* and predecessors such as David Hume,* had proceeded much more abstractly.

Nietzsche uses his vast cultural and historical knowledge to comment on several aspects of the contemporary moral Zeitgeist*(spirit of the times) and eventually succeeded in directing the interests of many of the most significant philosophers and thinkers who came after him. As the German poet and essayist Gottfried

> ❝ In reading Nietzsche's *Genealogy* one encounters an
> incomparable voice that has permeated many of the
> cultural dialogues of our age, a mind of great depth
> and ingenuity, and a literary masterpiece whose power,
> subtlety, wit, and attention to psychological detail repay
> almost endless close reading. ❞
>
> Christopher Janaway, *Beyond Selflessness*

Benn* remarked: "Virtually everything my generation discussed, tried to think through … had long been expressed and exhausted by Nietzsche."[1]

However, Nietzsche departs somewhat from his stated aim. In *Genealogy,* the proponents of the slave morality are associated with the Jews, and the noble morality with the Romans—"the strong and noble ones"—and specific events such as the Christianization of the Roman Empire are alluded to, in the process of which "Rome has succumbed without any doubt" to the slave morality. Yet it is never made clear exactly who the historical actors were, or when and where the events took place, and Nietzsche bases his claims on a general—though profound—familiarity with the historical literature, rather than giving a tight, evidenced narrative explicitly based on concrete sources. This may be partly because the slave revolt in morality took "two thousand years to achieve."[2]

Achievement in Context
Nietzsche suffered from health issues during the writing of *Genealogy,* notably digestive problems and frequent migraines that would leave him incapacitated for weeks. It is remarkable how much he was able to achieve despite these handicaps: as a Nietzsche scholar points out, "Lesser people under the same physical pressures might not have had

the inclination to pick up a pen".[3] Yet in a very short time Nietzsche produced a book that was hugely influential. Though Nietzsche had to finance the entire cost of the publication, and the text went on to sell very few copies during his lifetime, eventually his ideas exerted a tremendous influence over twentieth-century thought, both inside and outside academia.

Nietzsche's aims for his *Genealogy* were wildly ambitious: to dismantle contemporary morality, to undermine the influence of organized religion in general and Christianity in particular, to introduce a new view of humanity as driven by unconscious drives and impulses rather than rationality, and to introduce a new way of doing philosophy that was grounded in the history of cultures and languages and psychology. Given these rather grandiose aims of the text, successfully bringing the project to fruition represents a monumental intellectual achievement.

Limitations

One major element of *Genealogy* is Nietzsche's criticism of what he saw as a degenerate German culture. As such, many passages of the text—particularly the diatribes against the composer Richard Wagner* and other contemporary German figures in the third essay—may hold less direct relevance today. Yet despite the book being tied to its time and place in these ways, Nietzsche's broad themes have far more general applications: he warns us of the apparently dire consequences of scientism* (the high degree of confidence in the singular power of science to explain reality), egalitarianism (the political ideology that people should be equal), capitalism (the economic system defined by maximization of profit and a lifestyle revolving around the pursuit of money), the welfare state (a system in which the state protects its most economically vulnerable through the distribution of tax revenue), the "modern softening of feelings,"[4] and the "inhibiting influence that democratic prejudice exercises in the modern world"[5]—all issues with persisting social relevance that continue to be debated today.

Nietzsche's lack of social contact may have contributed to the eccentricity of some of his views, particularly in his attitude toward race, women, and sex,[6] and many of his remarks can seem outdated and even embarrassing to a modern reader. However, his distance from the academic establishment of his German homeland enabled him to develop ideas that are profoundly original. His deep interest in culture and the arts has been rewarded with a much broader readership than most philosophers could hope for; his philosophy has inspired later generations of philosophers, sociologists, and psychologists, as well as thinkers from all walks of cultural life, including dancers, novelists and, poets, painters, essayists, and social revolutionaries.[7]

NOTES

1   Gottfried Benn, "Nietzsche—nach 50 Jahren" in *Nietzsche und die deutsche Literatur*, ed. Bruno Hillebrand (Munich: Deutscher Taschenbuchverlag 1978).

2   Friedrich Nietzsche, *On the Genealogy of Morality*, trans. Maudemarie Clark and Alan Swensen (Indianapolis: Hackett Publishing Co., 1998), 17.

3   "Nietzsche's Life and Works," *Stanford Encyclopedia of Philosophy*, last modified March 17th, 2017, accessed April 25th, 2017, http://plato.stanford.edu/entries/nietzsche-life-works/.

4   Nietzsche, *Genealogy*, 5.

5   Nietzsche, *Genealogy*, 12.

6   Friedrich Nietzsche, *The Gay Science,* trans. Josefine Nauckhoff, ed. Bernard Williams (Cambridge: Cambridge University Press, 2001), introduction, ix.

7   "Nietzsche's Life and Works," *Stanford Encyclopedia of Philosophy*

MODULE 8
PLACE IN THE AUTHOR'S WORK

KEY POINTS

- The majority of Nietzsche's writings embody a deep concern with political and cultural rejuvenation, skepticism about the purported universality of moral ideals, and opposition to the stifling influence of religion.

- Nietzsche's attack on conventional morality had already begun prior to *Genealogy*, and he develops its themes further in later works.

- *Genealogy* is still among his most influential and most read works, and is often hailed as the most developed expression of his views on morality.

Positioning

Friedrich Nietzsche's *On the Genealogy of Morality* constitutes his most systematic examination of the themes it addresses, though they all arise in earlier works and are developed in later ones, and he had already put his genealogical method into practice on a smaller scale. The rejuvenation of German culture was a theme of Nietzsche's 1872 work *The Birth of Tragedy*, and in his 1878 book *Human, All Too Human* his views on Christian morality "found their first, economical, and preliminary expression."[1] *Daybreak* (1881) questions whether moral acts are necessarily selfless and unegoistic, and *The Gay Science* (1882) announces that "God is dead"[2] in reference to the declining influence of religion. This was followed in 1883 by *Thus Spoke Zarathustra*, a literary and allegorical work, full of biblical themes and images, in which Nietzsche begins to draw up new tables of the virtues.

The 1886 work *Beyond Good and Evil* is highly similar to *Genealogy*; indeed, the inside cover of *Genealogy* bore the words "Appended to

> ❝Because *Genealogy* was published in his penultimate productive year, it can largely be taken as Nietzsche's 'finished' thoughts on its major topics. During his final year, he himself called it 'my touchstone of what belongs to me,' thereby granting it the role of criterion for which of his earlier ideas still count as 'Nietzschean.'❞
>
> Maudemarie Clark, introduction to *On the Genealogy of Morality*

the recently published *Beyond Good and Evil* as a supplement and clarification."[3] In *Twilight of the Idols* (1888), Nietzsche reiterates that we cannot in good conscience retain a Christian morality without belief in God, and *The Anti-Christ* (1895), Nietzsche's most sustained attack on Christianity, gives "a concrete, historically more rooted version of themes treated in *On the Genealogy of Morality.*"[4]

Though Nietzsche did not seem to regard *Genealogy* as one of his most important works (in the autobiographical *Ecce Homo* he describes it as merely "a psychologist's three crucial preparatory works for a revaluation of all values"[5]—a project that was never completed), it has been among his most influential books and contains a definitive statement of his views on morality.

Integration

Nietzsche's short but productive career took a number of intellectual turns. In *The Birth of Tragedy*, Nietzsche regards art as "the highest task and the true metaphysical activity of this life";[6] yet by the 1878 work *Human, All too Human* he has come to see science as the highest human achievement, and its creation as "the most heroic story in the history of the human spirit."[7] By the time *Genealogy* was written, he was questioning the ideals of science: "Science itself now *is in need of* a justification (which is not to say that there is one)."[8] But in his later works *The Anti-Christ* and *Ecco Homo*, truth again becomes a central ideal: the question "How much truth can a spirit *tolerate?*" is regarded as "the real measure of value."[9]

Despite these radical changes of attitude toward fundamental questions, certain themes remain constant throughout. Nietzsche is perennially concerned with the limitations of traditional philosophy; the decline of culture; the foundations, cultural role, and later limitations of natural science; a skepticism about absolute values following the "death of God"; and what he takes to be the negative and stifling influence of Christianity. These themes serve to give Nietzsche's overall intellectual output an underlying unity.

Significance

Nietzsche's influence has changed considerably since the time his body of work was produced. Though he was relatively obscure during his own lifetime, the progress of serious Nietzsche scholarship in the English language since the German American philosopher Walter Kaufmann's* book *Nietzsche: Philosopher, Psychologist, Antichrist* (1950)—the "major event of twentieth-century Nietzsche scholarship in the United States"[10]—has shown many of his ideas to be of central relevance to contemporary concerns in analytic* philosophy.

In continental* philosophy, Nietzsche's work had already come to acquire a dominant position by the first half of the 20th Century, and has maintained this centrality ever since. His reputation has been enhanced by serious attention from leading continental thinkers such as the German philosopher Martin Heidegger,* the French philosopher Jean-Paul Sartre,* and the influential French historian of ideas and social theorist Michel Foucault.* Nietzsche's ideas about the subconscious received far more serious attention after being developed by the founder of psychoanalytical theory, Sigmund Freud,* and are now central to research in psychology.

As a book written close to the end of his career, *Genealogy* shows Nietzsche at the height of his intellectual powers. A writer elsewhere working in a highly terse and aphoristic form, swiftly moving from one theme to the next, in *Genealogy* he sets aside this eclectic style in order to pursue his themes in earnest. *Genealogy* is his "most extended discussion"[11] of morality, as well as of other topics such as perspectivism* (the idea that our understanding of the world is largely a product of our character, background experiences, interests, and attitudes).

NOTES

1   Friedrich Nietzsche, *On the Genealogy of Morality*, trans. Maudemarie Clark and Alan Swensen (Indianapolis: Hackett Publishing Co., 1998), 1.

2   Friedrich Nietzsche, *The Gay Science*, trans. Josefine Nauckhoff, ed. Bernard Williams (Cambridge: Cambridge University Press, 2001), 120.

3   Nietzsche, *Genealogy*, ii.

4   Friedrich Nietzsche, *The Anti-Christ, Ecce Homo, Twilight of the Idols. And Other Writings*, trans. Judith Norman, ed. Aaron Ridley (Cambridge: Cambridge University Press, 2005), introduction, ix.

5   Nietzsche, *Ecce Homo,* 136.

6   Friedrich Nietzsche, *The Birth of Tragedy and Other Writings*, trans. Ronald Speirs, ed. Raymond Geuss and Ronald Speirs (Cambridge: Cambridge University Press, 1999), 14.

7   Friedrich Nietzsche, *Human, All Too Human*, trans. and ed. R. J. Hollingdale (Cambridge: Cambridge University Press, 1996), 266.

8   Nietzsche, *Genealogy*, 110.

9   Nietzsche, *Ecce Homo*, 72.

10 Nietzsche, *Genealogy*, xi.

11 Nietzsche, *Genealogy*, xv.

SECTION 3
IMPACT

MODULE 9
THE FIRST RESPONSES

KEY POINTS

- Contemporary criticisms of Nietzsche's work tended to be based on misunderstandings.

- There were no genuine responses to the text in Nietzsche's lifetime.

- It would be many years before his views were properly understood and he would be recognized as a respected philosopher.

Criticism

The initial reception of Friedrich Nietzsche's works, *On the Genealogy of Morality* among them, was nothing short of disastrous. Due to its unusual focus and lack of conventional academic tools such as citations, his first book, *On the Birth of Tragedy*, published in 1872, received a scathing review from Ulrich von Wilamowitz-Möllendorff,* the most influential German classical scholar of his era. Möllendorff was "harshly critical" of the work, and indeed "dismissive of Nietzsche's whole project,"[1] correctly regarding the text as more akin to art or philosophy than a scholarly work of philological science.* This destroyed Nietzsche's reputation as a promising young classical scholar, and his subsequent books received very little attention upon their publication, especially within his native Germany. Upon his completion of *On the Genealogy of Morality* in November 1887, Nietzsche was forced to pay the publication costs himself, and the text was only circulated among a handful of friends and acquaintances.

We can, however, get some indication of the contemporary reaction by looking at reviews of his two previous books, to which

> ❝ Serious health problems, undoubtedly exacerbated by his increasing feeling of being unsuited to the life of academic scholarship, forced him to resign his chair in 1879, allowing him to escape and begin life anew as a writer of philosophy. The first five books he published in this new role, however—*Human, All Too Human*; *Daybreak*; *The Gay Science*; *Thus Spoke Zarathustra*; and *Beyond Good and Evil*—sold so few copies that no publisher would touch his *Genealogy*. ❞
>
> Maudemarie Clark, introduction to *On the Genealogy of Morality*

Nietzsche's *Genealogy* was intended as a "supplement and clarification".[2] In the daily Swiss newspaper *Der Bund*, the Swiss poet Carl Spitteler* published a review of Nietzsche's *Thus Spoke Zarathustra*, regarding it merely as a "superior stylistic exercise,"[3] entirely missing its jubilant philosophical message. Joseph Viktor Widmann,* the editor of the same paper, published a review of *Beyond Good and Evil* entitled "Nietzsche's Dangerous Book,"[4] wherein he suggested Nietzsche was trying to "do away with all decent feelings,"[5] and sought to warn others against what he regarded as the potentially harmful consequences of Nietzsche's attack on conventional morality.

Responses

After retiring from his teaching position at the University of Basel in 1879 for health reasons, Nietzsche spent the following decade largely in isolation from academic life. Moreover, he suffered a permanent mental breakdown in January 1889, just over a year after the publication of *On the Genealogy of Morality*. For these reasons, there was very little opportunity for him to form an active relationship with his critics during his lifetime. He did, however, write the autobiographical work *Ecce Homo*, one of the five books written between *Genealogy* and his untimely collapse, which enables us to speculate about the responses he might have given to criticism.

In a section entitled "Why I Write Such Good Books," Nietzsche reflects upon the words of his critics, responding briefly to charges of idealism* (the view that reality is a mental construct) and Darwinism* (that it viewed history solely in terms of Charles Darwin's* theory of natural selection*). He does this, however, only "with all the carelessness it warrants"[6], the irreverent tone of this remark conveying his awareness that contemporary readers would inevitably misunderstand his work. His attitude toward this is clearly one of indifference, and he expresses the view that, ultimately, "nobody can get more out of things—including books—than they already know."[7] For Nietzsche, his reviewers were simply unsuited to receiving his profoundly original ideas. For this reason, he asks that we "forgive my complete lack of curiosity about reviews of my books."[8]

Conflict and Consensus

The formation of a consensus on Nietzsche's *Genealogy* was a complex event. Though he was an obscure figure during his own lifetime, he harbored hopes for his growing readership in "Vienna, in St Petersburg, in Stockholm, in Copenhagen, in Paris and New York,"[9] where the intellectual climate was better suited to his ideas. He was even made the subject of a series of lectures by the influential Danish scholar Georg Brandes,* delivered at the University of Copenhagen in 1888. Yet it would not be until the following decade that his name was truly rescued from "the absurd silence under which it lies buried"[10] by his sister Elizabeth Förster-Nietzsche,* who achieved fame for her brother's work only at the expense of unfairly associating it with the fascist and genocidal Nazi* regime that governed Germany between 1933 and 1945.

Though Nietzsche has always been a central figure in the continental* philosophical traditions, he was not at first taken seriously in Anglophone analytic* philosophy. He was, for example, curtly dismissed by the English philosopher Bertrand Russell* in his *History of Western Philosophy* (1945). The German American scholar Walter Kaufmann later rehabilitated Nietzsche as a reputable philosopher only by presenting his ideas as more conventional than they are, but since then substantial interest by renowned philosophers such as the British thinkers Bernard Williams* and Alasdair MacIntyre* has led to the consensus view of his *Genealogy* as a highly original and ultimately highly influential work in moral theory and the history of ideas.

NOTES

1   Friedrich Nietzsche, *The Birth of Tragedy and Other Writings*, trans. Ronald Speirs, ed. Raymond Geuss and Ronald Speirs (Cambridge: Cambridge University Press, 1999), introduction, xxviii.

2   Friedrich Nietzsche, *On the Genealogy of Morality,* trans. Maudemarie Clark and Alan Swensen (indianapolis: Hackett Publishing Co., 1998), ii.

3   Friedrich Nietzsche, *The Anti-Christ, Ecce Homo, Twilight of the Idols. And Other Writings*, trans. Judith Norman, ed. Aaron Ridley (Cambridge: Cambridge University Press, 2005) 100.

4   Joseph Viktor Widmann, "Nietzsche's Dangerous Book," *New Nietzsche Studies* 4 (2000): 195–200.

5   Nietzsche, *Ecce Homo*, 101.

6   Nietzsche, *Ecce Homo,* 100.

7   Nietzsche, *Ecce Homo,* 101.

8   Nietzsche, *Ecce Homo*, 101.

9   Friedrich Nietzsche, *On the Genealogy of Morality*, 102.

10 Nietzsche, *Ecce Homo,* 143.

MODULE 10
THE EVOLVING DEBATE

KEY POINTS

- Nietzsche's works and his *Genealogy* in particular have been a central influence on a significant number of schools of thought that emerged in the twentieth century.

- The text contributed to the emergence of existentialism,* postmodernism,* and psychoanalysis.*

- Most writers in the continental* philosophical tradition have been deeply influenced by Nietzsche. The French thinker Michel Foucault* followed Nietzsche's genealogical method in writing histories of sexuality, madness, and punishment.

Uses and Problems

Friedrich Nietzsche and his text *On the Genealogy of Morality* have had a profound influence on many central figures in twentieth-century intellectual life, including: the psychologist Sigmund Freud,* who was influenced by Nietzsche's ideas about subconscious motivation and the repression of the darker side of human nature through civilization; the Irish playwright George Bernard Shaw,* whose play *Man and Superman* (1903) was inspired by Nietzsche's concept of the Übermensch;* and the Irish novelist James Joyce,* who gave expression to Nietzsche's doctrine of perspectivism* in his 1922 novel *Ulysses*.[1] But perhaps the intellectual tradition that Nietzsche has influenced most is continental* philosophy, where his ideas have given direction to the thought of central figures such as the German thinker Martin Heidegger* and the French philosopher and cultural critic Gilles Deleuze,* each of whom has produced book-length studies of

> ❝ Nietzsche, more than any other philosopher of the past hundred years, represents a major historical event. His ideas are of concern not only to the members of one nation or community, nor alone to philosophers, but to men everywhere, and they have had repercussions in recent history and literature as well as in psychology and religious thought. ❞
>
> Walter Kaufmann, *Nietzsche: Philosopher, Psychologist, Antichrist*

his philosophy.

Perhaps the name most associated with the term "genealogy" in Nietzsche's sense is Michel Foucault, who gives an analysis of Nietzsche's method in a 1977 paper entitled "Nietzsche, Genealogy, History."[2] A thinker who traversed the boundaries between historiography (the study of historical method), philosophy, and social theory, Foucault also wrote influential histories of sexuality (1976 onward) and madness (1961) that draw on Nietzsche's techniques, and a book called *Discipline and Punish* (1975) that builds on Nietzsche's ideas about punishment in *Genealogy*.[3] When interviewed in 1982, Foucault asserted firmly that "Nietzsche was a revelation to me."[4]

Schools of Thought

Nietzsche's *Genealogy* has influenced schools of thought as diverse as Marxism* (a political philosophy emphasising the economics forces shaping society, pioneered by the German social theorist Karl Marx)* and feminism* (an intellectual and political movement that seeks to bring about the end of sexual discrimination); however, those most associated with his name are existentialism,* postmodernism,* and psychoanalysis.*

Existentialism is a twentieth-century philosophical and literary movement centered on the philosophy of Jean-Paul Sartre,* though its roots lay with Nietzsche and the Danish philosopher Søren Kierkegaard.* It addresses the Nietzschean theme of the radical new freedom we possess after the "death of God" (the post-Enlightenment* decline of religious influence on many aspects of life, including culture, politics, and art) and the subsequent need for us to create our own values. It also follows Nietzsche's advice of writing philosophy that has a connection to lived human experience, and which is emotive and personal, rather than abstract and aspiring to universality.

In philosophy, postmodernism is most associated with the Nietzschean themes of the problematic nature of truth and interpretation, and the fundamental importance of power. Nietzsche's approach to the analysis of key concepts in *Genealogy* has become a central tool among many of the movement's practitioners other than Foucault, and his doctrine of perspectivism discussed in the third essay has also been highly influential.

Lastly, the psychoanalytic movement comprises both psychological theory and a therapeutic methodology based on ideas explored in *Genealogy*: that the self is composed of primitive and competing drives that are partially repressed through culture, and that these unconscious, irrational drives are the true motivating causes of human behavior. Its founder, Sigmund Freud,* wrote of Nietzsche that "he had a more penetrating knowledge of himself than any man who ever lived or was likely to live."[5]

In Current Scholarship

The continental philosopher Gilles Deleuze claimed that "modern philosophy has largely lived off Nietzsche,"[6] and unifying features of continental philosophy—such as its historical emphasis—can often be traced back to him. However, the influence of his *Genealogy* in analytic* philosophy has been less profound, and the subject is still largely ahistorical. Yet even here there are philosophers such as Maudemarie Clarke,* Brian Leiter, John Richardson, and Christopher

Janaway* who are primarily known as Nietzsche scholars, focusing on historical and interpretive questions relating to his work, and publishing their findings in dedicated journals such as *New Nietzsche Studies.*

A number of analytic philosophers have also attempted to follow Nietzsche's *Genealogy* with related projects. The influential moral philosopher Bernard Williams's* 2002 book *Truth and Truthfulness* bears the subtitle "An Essay in Genealogy," and in it he uses the genealogical method to justify the Enlightenment ideal of truthfulness, commenting that the "problems that concern this book were discovered, effectively, by Nietzsche."[7]

Like Nietzsche, the Scottish moral philosopher Alasdair MacIntyre* also proceeds in a deeply historical vein, and follows Nietzsche in regarding the Enlightenment project of rationally justifying morality as unworkable. He views Nietzsche as a pivotal figure because of his "relentlessly serious pursuit"[8] of this problem. However, for MacIntyre, Nietzsche was himself limited by the individualist assumptions of his social order, and MacIntyre contends that what is now needed is a return to a much older tradition stemming from the ancient Greek philosopher Aristotle.*

NOTES

1   Joseph Valente, "Beyond Truth and Freedom: The New Faith of Joyce and Nietzsche," *James Joyce Quarterly* 25 (1987): 87–103.

2   Michel Foucault, "Nietzsche, Genealogy, History," in *Language, Counter-Memory, Practice: Selected Essays and Interviews by Michel Foucault*, trans. Donald F. Bouchard and Sherry Simon, ed. Donald F. Bouchard (Oxford: Blackwell, 1977).

3   See Michel Foucault, *The History of Sexuality*, vols. 1–3, trans. Robert Hurley (London: Allen Lane, 1978–86); Foucault, *History of Madness,* trans. Jonathan Murphy and Jean Khalfa, ed. Jean Khalfa (London: Routledge, 2006); Foucault, *Discipline and Punish: The Birth of the Prison*, trans. Alan Sheridan (New York: Pantheon Books, 1977).

4   "Truth, Power, Self: An Interview with Michel Foucault, October 25 1982," in *Technologies of the Self: A Seminar with Michel Foucault*, ed. L. H. Martin et al. (London: Tavistock Press, 1988), 9–15.

5   Ernest Jones, *The Life and Work of Sigmund Freud*, vol. 2II (New York: Basic Books, 1953), 344.

6   Gilles Deleuze, *Nietzsche and Philosophy*, trans. H. Tomlinson (London: Athlone Press, 1983).

7   Bernard Williams. *Truth and Truthfulness: An Essay in Genealogy* (Princeton: Princeton University Press, 2002), 12–13.

8   Alasdair MacIntyre, *After Virtue* (London: Bloomsbury, 2011), 133.

MODULE 11
IMPACT AND INFLUENCE TODAY

KEY POINTS

- Nietzsche's texts, and *On the Genealogy of Morality* in particular, are now widely read among those studying in Anglo-American and European philosophy departments.

- Nietzsche challenges both our contemporary moral ideals and the ahistorical way in which moral philosophy is still practiced by many philosophers today.

- Some claim Nietzsche has committed the genetic fallacy* by equating questions about the current value of an idea with questions as to its origin.

Position

Friedrich Nietzsche's *On the Genealogy of Morality* continues to play an important role in contemporary philosophy. This is especially true in the continental* tradition, where the ideas it contains still serve to inspire the work of key thinkers. For instance, one of the many well-known contemporary German philosophers who have been greatly influenced by Nietzsche is Peter Sloterdijk,* who follows *Genealogy's* imperative that a philosopher must stand outside the contemporary moral culture, at a distance from received views, in order to better criticize them, rather than simply giving these conventions a systematic expression. As Sloterdijk himself puts it: "It is no accident that the great representatives of critique—the French moralists, the Encyclopaedists, the socialists, and especially Heine, Marx, Nietzsche, and Freud—remain outsiders to the scholarly domain."[1]

In university analytic* philosophy departments, Nietzsche's *Genealogy* is regularly given as a text to be read for students of moral philosophy and nineteenth-century philosophy. Yet although most

> ❝ It is thus nothing short of amazing that at the end
> of the twentieth century, *On the Genealogy of Morality*
> stands as a widely acknowledged masterpiece. Many
> consider it indispensable reading for understanding the
> intellectual life of the twentieth century, and some (a
> smaller group certainly) consider it essential reading for
> anyone who is serious about understanding morality. In
> the United States, at least, the book is now often taught
> in standard ethics courses at some of the best colleges
> and universities. ❞
>
> Maudemarie Clark, introduction to *On the Genealogy of Morality*

analytic philosophers are familiar with his central contentions, they
have largely ignored his attacks on established Western moral ideals,
and simply continued with the Enlightenment* project of justifying
our inherited moral framework, overlooking the challenge to this
project that Nietzsche has thrown down. Unlike in continental
philosophy, where many thinkers such as Michel Foucault* have
followed his methodology and style directly, the text is not used to
offer an example for how philosophy should now be written.

Interaction

Nietzsche challenges contemporary analytic moral philosophy in at
least two ways. The first is to dispute the equation of virtue and
selflessness. Referring to selfish desires, the English moral philosopher
Bernard Williams* writes that the "contrast between these
considerations and the ethical is a platitude,"[2] and this is the attitude of
most moral philosophers today. Yet for Nietzsche, this is just one of a
number of possible moral outlooks. His work also embodies a critique
of liberal and egalitarian values (that is, values based on notions of
liberty and equality); for him our highest concern lies with the

development of strong, independent, and creative individuals like the poet and playwright Johann Wolfgang von Goethe* and the composer Ludwig van Beethoven.* He insists that this goal requires both a strictly hierarchical society and an open awareness of this hierarchy. His text is, therefore, a powerful expression of an elitist, aristocratic outlook that challenges contemporary values.

Second, Nietzsche also challenges the project of giving a rational foundation to morality in favor of a more nuanced and historically sensitive approach. Moral philosophers working in the analytic tradition today typically proceed by beginning with a set of intuitive and partially articulated moral judgments and attempt to systemize them and give them a rational foundation. This process takes place without reference to concrete history, as practitioners regard themselves as addressing timeless, perennial questions. But Nietzsche rejects this approach, instead stressing the historically situated nature of moral questions and the range of conflicting and intersecting forces underlying our current moral thoughts and feelings, which require detailed historical study to be brought to light.

The Continuing Debate

In a famous paper titled "Nietzsche's Immoralism" (1993),[3] the British philosopher Philippa Foot* rebukes what she takes to be Nietzsche's hostility toward acting morally. But more detailed scholarly attention reveals that Nietzsche is not opposed to morality as such, merely to the Judeo-Christian* interpretation of morality—which he reveals as only one of many frameworks for ethical life. He is also more concerned with the foundations of morality than reorienting our everyday actions: "It goes without saying that I do not deny—unless I am a fool—that many actions called immoral ought to be avoided and resisted, or that many called moral ought to be done and encouraged."[4]

Another typical response is to attack Nietzsche's inherent historicism:* the view that historical methods provide our best chance of reaching sound conclusions. Writing about the philosopher Alasdair MacIntyre's* *After Virtue*, the American moral philosopher William K. Frankena* objected that "I can, if I have the right conceptual equipment, understand *what* the view is without seeing it as the result of a historical development; and, so far as I can see, I can also assess its status as true or false or rational to believe without seeing it as such an outcome."[5] But Nietzsche's reasons for adopting a historical approach to morality are partly rhetorical rather than logical: historical inquiry makes it psychologically possible for us to question moral assumptions that had formerly been largely unconscious.

NOTES

1 Peter Sloterdijk, *Critique of Cynical Reason* (Minnesota: University of Minnesota Press, 1988), 18.

2 Bernard Williams, *Ethics and the Limits of Philosophy* (Abingdon: Routledge, 2011), 13.

3 Philippa Foot, "Nietzsche's Immoralism," in *Nietzsche, Genealogy, Morality: Essays on Nietzsche's Genealogy of Morals*, ed. Richard Schacht (Berkeley: University of California Press, 1994).

4 Friedrich Nietzsche, *Daybreak*, trans. R. J. Hollingdale, ed. Maudemarie Clark and Brian Leiter (Cambridge: Cambridge University Press, 1997), 103.

5 William K. Frankena, "Review: MacIntyre and Modern Morality," *Ethics* 93 (1983): 500.

MODULE 12
WHERE NEXT?

KEY POINTS

- Nietzsche's text will surely continue to influence future generations of thinkers inside and outside philosophy.

- *On the Genealogy of Morality* continues to throw down a challenge to those who still hold as true the moral views it so relentlessly attacks.

- With its unrivaled lucidity and poetic imagination, the book remains the most profound expression of the provocative and controversial views it contains.

Potential

As the most systematic expression of Friedrich Nietzsche's mature views on morality and other topics, his 1887 text *On the Genealogy of Morality* is a book whose central place in moral philosophy and its wide readership outside of it appear secure. Though in analytic* philosophy there has been a steady increase in Nietzsche studies since his rehabilitation as a reputable philosopher in the 1950s, in many ways a convincing response to his challenge is yet to appear. Moral philosophy in the Anglophone tradition has yet to react to Nietzsche's charges of being too abstract and ahistorical, still stands in a precarious relation to contemporary science, and still struggles to distance itself from its religious origins.

In all cultures where the influence of religion has declined but where no new values have been put forth to replace those moral ideals we have inherited, it is still Nietzsche who gives the clearest expression to many of the cultural and intellectual problems we now face. Moreover, the strategies he uses to approach them in *Genealogy* are so

> ❝The problem then is how to construct in an entirely original way, how to invent a new table of what is good and a law, a problem which arises for each individual. This problem would constitute the core of a Nietzschean moral philosophy. For it is in his relentlessly serious pursuit of the problem, not in his frivolous solutions that Nietzsche's greatness lies, the greatness that makes him *the* moral philosopher *if* the only alternatives to Nietzsche's moral philosophy turn out to be those formulated by the philosophers of the Enlightenment and their successors.❞
>
> Alasdair MacIntyre, *After Virtue*

richly suggestive that the text is certain to continue to inspire defenses of the doctrines it attacks: doctrines that still claim a place at the heart of moral life in the twenty-first century.

Future Directions

There are many contemporary schools of thought that could stand to learn from Nietzsche—for instance, the contemporary strand of naturalism* deriving from the English philosopher Edward Craig's* 1990 text *Knowledge and the State of Nature*.

In this work, Craig pursues an account of the concept of knowledge that is broadly pragmatist—that is, it considers how the concept is used in concrete situations in our everyday lives. Craig's approach is in many ways similar to the approach of the thinkers Nietzsche called the "English psychologists."* He begins from a hypothesis about the concept of knowledge—that it is "used to flag approved sources of information"[1] by identifying individuals likely to give us the right answer regarding any question we might need to know the answer to. Nietzsche's criticisms of Paul Rée* and others to explaining the origins of morality and our institutions of punishment—that is, through attributing to them a singular purpose—therefore apply equally to this contemporary project, too.

Another relevant development is in moral philosophy, where in recent decades an Aristotelian* "virtue ethics" position has become a third popular option alongside views derived from the work of Immanuel Kant* and the utilitarian* philosophers Jeremy Bentham* and John Stuart Mill.* Nietzsche's moral philosophy is closer to Aristotle's than is usually acknowledged: both take character traits and human lives in their entirety as of the greatest importance, and while for Aristotle the virtues—courage and justice, for example—receive their rational justification as being those traits that move us closer to a condition of *eudaemonia** (flourishing or living the good life), Nietzsche also insists we ask of our values: "Have they inhibited or furthered human flourishing up until now?"[2]

However, an Aristotelian account of human nature implies that human flourishing is largely a matter of the quality of the relationships we enjoy with others. Nietzsche's radical individualism challenges this picture, suggesting that further engagement between Nietzscheans and Aristotelians would be a fruitful future development.

Summary

On the Genealogy of Morality shows Nietzsche at his very best. In it he manages to artfully combine acute skepticism, rigor, and precision with vivid imagery, metaphor, sensitivity, humor, passion, and irony, and it has surely contributed to his reputation as an exceptional writer of German prose. It also gives the most extended discussion of the themes that were closest to him, particularly our concepts of "good" and "evil," the origins of the moral conscience, and how human beings might best decide to live their lives. With his deep knowledge of history, Western culture, and classical literature, Nietzsche has written a text that has inspired poets, novelists, painters, psychologists, and dissident political figures, as well as philosophers.

The restless and relentless struggle to break free of established values and methods, and even of his own previous writings, that is embodied in Nietzsche's *Genealogy* cost him both his academic career and many of his personal relationships. However, the fruits of his labors are clear: in a relatively short book readers are taken on a journey that enables them to call into question their deepest-held values, as these are at last recognized as the outcome of a historical process that was previously unacknowledged.

Nietzsche's unique position at the very edge of the social and moral culture of his time enabled him to develop ideas of such striking originality that his *Genealogy*'s central place in moral philosophy has been permanently secured.

NOTES

1   Edward Craig, *Knowledge and the State of Nature: An Essay in Conceptual Synthesis* (Oxford: Oxford University Press, 1990).

2   Friedrich Nietzsche, *On the Genealogy of Morality*, trans. Maudemarie Clark and Alan Swensen (Indianapolis: Hackett Publishing Co., 1998), 2–3.

GLOSSARY

GLOSSARY OF TERMS

Analytic philosophy: a style of philosophy that has in the last century come to dominate university departments in the English-speaking world. It has its roots in the logical tradition of the German mathematician and philosopher Gottlob Frege (1848–1925), and the English founders of the movement, Bertrand Russell (1872–1970) and G. E. Moore (1873–1958). It emphasizes clarity, literal expression, rigorous rational argument, and the study of language and meaning.

Continental philosophy: a diverse set of nineteenth- and twentieth-century philosophical traditions united by an interest in the historical and cultural variability of answers to philosophical questions, the limitations of purely scientific modes of inquiry, and the possibility of mobilizing philosophical theory to achieve practical goals.

Empirical: relating to direct observation or sensory experience. A proposition is empirical if it needs to be justified by investigation into the physical world.

English psychologists: Nietzsche uses this phrase to refer to a group of naturalists who sought to reduce human experiences to mechanical phenomena, later making use of the theory of evolution by natural selection supplied by Charles Darwin. "English" denotes a cultural stereotype: the tradition includes thinkers of various nationalities.

Enlightenment: an important historical period in Western civilization that began roughly in the middle of the seventeenth century and continued throughout the eighteenth century. It was characterized by dramatic revolutions in the sciences—culminating in the work of the extremely influential physicist Sir Isaac Newton—and in philosophy, where increasing confidence was placed in the power of reason and rational argumentation.

Etymology: the study of words and their origins and changes of meaning over time.

Eudaemonia: the state of living well, often translated as "flourishing," "happiness," or "well-being." In Aristotelian philosophy, living organisms move toward *eudaemonia* by pursuing their *telos* (or highest end).

Existentialism: a twentieth-century philosophical and literary movement centered on individual human subjects and their experiences and relationship to the world around them. It is most strongly associated with the philosopher Jean-Paul Sartre.

Feminism: an intellectual and political movement that seeks to effect the end of sexual discrimination, and pursues inquiries into such discrimination in relation to issues such as the body, class, employment, reproduction, race, science, human rights, and popular culture.

Genealogy: a continuous history of the descent or development of some person or phenomenon.

Genetic fallacy: the mistaken view that in coming to understand the origins of something we have therefore settled the question of its current value.

German materialists: a group of thinkers who espoused a materialist doctrine (that is, the doctrine that only physical objects exist). The most important of these was the German philosopher Ludwig Feuerbach (1804–72), known for his criticisms of religion and idealism.

Historicism: either the view that only history itself can provide us with rational standards for thought or the position that our best chance of attaining truth in some particular area of inquiry is by employing historical methods.

Idealism: the metaphysical view that reality is somehow mental in nature, and the most fundamental reality consists of ideas or mind.

Judeo-Christian morality: the shared moral inheritance of the Judaic and Christian traditions, as embodied in the Ten Commandments and the teachings of the Old Testament.

Lutheranism: a branch of Christianity that stems from the theological doctrines of Martin Luther (1483–1546), a German monk and Catholic priest whose challenge to the authority of the pope helped catalyze the Protestant Reformation.

Marxism: both a methodology for sociological analysis and a theory of historical development. Inspired by the writings of Karl Marx, its traditional emphasis has been on class conflict, the economic determination of behavior, and a systematic and trenchant critique of the capitalist (that is, profit-oriented) economy.

Materialism: the doctrine that only physical objects exist.

Natural selection: a process by which species change over time. Random genetic mutations occasionally cause a member of a species to be better adapted to its environment, which makes it more likely to survive and pass on the advantageous genes to the next generation.

Naturalism: an approach to inquiry that considers only natural— rather than supernatural— causes of phenomena.

Nazi: The German political party founded by Adolf Hitler in 1919. Nazi is short for *Nationalsozialismus* (National Socialism). The party controlled Germany (and increasingly large parts of Europe) until the end of World War II in 1945.

Perspectivism: the view that the world looks essentially different depending on our character, background experiences, interests, and attitudes, and moreover that there are no reasons to privilege any one of these points of view over another. Particular interpretations of phenomena can thus only come to dominate by force.

Philology: the branch of knowledge dealing with natural languages and their historical development, especially with reference to classical literature.

Postmodernism: a complex intellectual movement associated with the socially constructed nature of truth and interpretation, the importance of power and its expression in social structures, and attempts to destabilize traditional binary oppositions.

Protestantism: one of the three principal branches of the Christian faith. Protestantism differs from Roman Catholicism, out of which it emerged, in its interpretation of scripture and in the nature of its rituals. It was largely inspired by the German theologian Martin Luther (1483–1546).

Prussia: a central European state that later became part of a unified Germany.

Psychoanalysis: both a psychological theory and a therapeutic methodology founded on the idea that unconscious, irrational drives are the true causes of human behavior.

Ressentiment: the French *ressentiment*, related to the English word "resentment," denotes a kind of repressed anger at one's situation later directed outward toward others. A key concept for Nietzsche, it was taken up by later theorists such as Sigmund Freud in discussions of unconscious, irrational drives.

Romanticism: a Western intellectual movement that began in the late eighteenth century and continued through to the mid-nineteenth century. It influenced contemporary literature, painting, music, architecture, historiography, and philosophy. It is often understood as a reaction to Enlightenment doctrines such as materialism and rationalism, instead emphasizing emotion, creativity, imagination, and individuality.

Scientism: a confidence in the authority of science and in the power of the scientific method to discover objective truths about the world—especially when the results of this inquiry conflict with other sources of belief, such as religious texts or abstract philosophical reasoning.

Sublimation: the process of transforming a desire into one that is more socially acceptable. This is a key concept in psychoanalysis.

Übermensch: traditionally translated "superman" or "overman," this is Nietzsche's term for the strong, independent, creative individuals, capable of creating new values, whom he hoped would arise in the future.

Utilitarianism: an ethical theory that claims that the moral worth of actions should be evaluated solely in terms of their impact on the overall happiness of everyone in society. Its founder, Jeremy Bentham, asserted that "it is the greatest happiness of the greatest number that is the measure of right and wrong."

Zeitgeist: literally German for "spirit of the time." This word denotes the spirit, mood, and popular ideas that define the people of a particular cultural or historical period.

PEOPLE MENTIONED IN THE TEXT

Aristotle (384–322 B.C.E.) was an ancient Greek philosopher. He wrote treatises on a vast range of subjects in both the arts and sciences, and pioneered the systematic study of biology and formal logic. His philosophy and cosmology dominated the intellectual landscape of the West for many centuries in the Middle Ages. In terms of influence, only Plato rivals him.

Ludwig van Beethoven (1770–1827) was a celebrated German composer and pianist. He wrote many of his most admired works while suffering from a loss of hearing that would become complete by the last decade of his life.

Gottfried Benn (1886–1956) was a German poet and essayist.

Jeremy Bentham (1748–1832) was a British philosopher and social reformer. He is chiefly known for being an early proponent of utilitarianism, the view that we should always pursue the "greatest happiness of the greatest number."

Otto von Bismarck (1815–98) was prime minister of Prussia and the first chancellor of the German Empire. After establishing the empire in 1871 his pragmatic foreign policies enabled him to keep the peace in Europe for two decades, though he was criticized for his authoritarian domestic reforms.

Georg Brandes (1842–1927) was an influential Danish critic and scholar. He was among the first to lecture on Nietzsche's work.

Maudemarie Clark is a professor of philosophy at the University of California, Riverside, and a prolific Nietzsche scholar.

Edward Craig (b. 1942) is a retired Cambridge philosopher and cricketer. He was the editor of the ten-volume *Routledge Encyclopedia of Philosophy*.

Charles Darwin (1809–82) was an English naturalist. He is most famous for being the first to articulate scientifically the proposition that all life is descended from a single source in a process that is driven by the mechanisms of natural selection. His work influenced virtually all aspects of the biological sciences.

Gilles Deleuze (1925–95) was an influential French philosopher. He attempted to develop a new metaphysical system that could accommodate the complexities of contemporary mathematics and science.

Denis Diderot (1713–84) was a philosopher of the French Enlightenment. He is best known for being the chief editor of the *Encyclopédie*, an attempt to set out systematically all the world's scientific knowledge, and for his many plays, poems, and novels, such as *Rameau's Nephew*.

Fyodor Dostoevsky (1821–81) was an acclaimed Russian novelist. He is best known for his psychologically penetrating portrayal of dark emotions, and for his long novels such as *Crime and Punishment* (1886).

Ralph Waldo Emerson (1803–82) was an American essayist and poet. He was a leading proponent of New England Transcendentalism, an idealist philosophical movement based on belief in the innate goodness of man and the primacy of intuition over rational methods.

Philippa Foot (1920–2010) was a British philosopher. She was a noted proponent of virtue ethics, a tradition stemming from Aristotle.

Elizabeth Förster-Nietzsche (1846–1935) was Nietzsche's sister. For many years she was the sole executor of his literary estate.

Michel Foucault (1926–84) was a French philosopher and social theorist. Heavily influenced by Nietzsche, he wrote extensively about power and its expression by social institutions through time. He also wrote histories of madness, sexuality, and punishment.

William K. Frankena (1908–94) was an American moral philosopher who worked in the analytic tradition; his main research interest was ethics.

Sigmund Freud (1856–1939) was an influential Austrian psychologist and medical doctor. He is best known as the founder of psychoanalysis, a school with both theoretical and therapeutic doctrines, that stressed the importance of unconscious, irrational drives and the experiences of childhood.

Johann Wolfgang von Goethe (1749–1832) was an influential German writer and politician. He is best known for his tragic play *Faust*.

Martin Heidegger (1889–1976) was an important German philosopher. He is associated with the phenomenological and existentialist traditions, and best known for his masterpiece *Being and Time*.

David Hume (1711–76) was an influential Scottish philosopher. He is known for his skeptical attitude toward received beliefs in philosophy and religion, his development of empiricism, and his attempts to ground metaphysical principles in human nature and habit rather than rational argumentation.

Christopher Janaway is professor of philosophy at the University of Southampton. He has published work on Schopenhauer and Nietzsche.

James Joyce (1882–1941) was an Irish novelist. Perhaps the most acclaimed novelist of the twentieth century, he is best known for his stream-of-consciousness prose style and his novels *Ulysses* and *Finnegan's Wake*.

Immanuel Kant (1724–1804) was a German Enlightenment philosopher. A towering figure in modern philosophy, he contributed to a wide range of areas including ethics, epistemology, metaphysics, and aesthetics, and sought to synthesize the rationalist and empiricist traditions of the early modern period.

Walter Kaufmann (1921–80) was a German-American philosopher, translator, and noted Nietzsche scholar. He provided many of the first translations of Nietzsche's key works, and was instrumental in the increasing interest in his writings from the mid-twentieth century onward.

Søren Kierkegaard (1813–55) was a Danish philosopher, theologian, and social critic. A founder of existentialism, he was interested in concrete human experiences and attempted to rejuvenate the Christian faith.

Friedrich Albert Lange (1828–75) was a German philosopher. He was instrumental in the development of neo-Kantianism and German social democratic thought.

Alasdair MacIntyre (b. 1929) is an influential Scottish philosopher. He is primarily known for his historical approach to moral philosophy, his Aristotelian and Thomistic commitments, and his trenchant critiques of liberal values.

Karl Marx (1818–83) was a highly influential economist and social theorist. Marxist theory is derived from his works, notably *Capital* (1867–94) and *The Communist Manifesto* (1848).

John Stuart Mill (1806–73) was an English philosopher and important liberal thinker. He is best known for his development of utilitarianism, but also made contributions to the philosophy of science and served as a member of parliament.

Paul Rée (1849–1901) was a philosopher and contemporary of Nietzsche. The two had previously been friends, though Nietzsche felt Rée had betrayed him over the affections of Lou Andreas-Salomé.

Friedrich Wilhelm Ritschl (1806–76) was a German classical scholar. He is most notable for his work on the Roman playwright Plautus.

François de La Rochefoucauld (1613–80) was a classical French author, nobleman, and political activist. He is primarily known for his *maximes*: short aphorisms containing a witty or polemical observation concerning some social or philosophical topic.

Bertrand Russell (1872–1970) was a British mathematician, social critic, and philosopher. He is regarded as one of the founders of the analytical school of philosophy.

Jean-Paul Sartre (1905–80) was a well-known French philosopher, writer, and public intellectual. In philosophy he is best known as the founder of the existentialist movement.

Arthur Schopenhauer (1788–1860) was a German philosopher, best known for his 1818 book *The World as Will and Representation*. Generally regarded as a pessimistic nihilist, he advocated the use of culture and the arts as an escape from the suffering inherent in human existence.

George Bernard Shaw (1856–1950) was an Irish dramatist and literary critic. In 1925 he won the Nobel Prize for Literature.

Peter Sloterdijk (b. 1947) is a German philosopher, cultural critic, and television presenter. His magnum opus *Spheres* is a three-volume work about the spaces in which human beings attempt to live.

Adam Smith (1723–90) was a philosopher and economist of the Scottish Enlightenment. He is primarily known for his 1776 work *An Inquiry into the Nature and Causes of the Wealth of Nations*, the first systematic treatise on political economy.

Herbert Spencer (1820–1903) was an English philosopher. He was an important exponent of evolutionary theory and utilitarian ideas.

Benedict Spinoza (1632–77) was a Dutch Jewish philosopher. He was one of the foremost exponents of rationalism and a central figure in the Enlightenment philosophical movement.

Carl Spitteler (1845–1924) was a Swiss poet. In recognition of his epic poem *Olympian Spring* he was awarded the Nobel Prize for Literature in 1919.

Richard Wagner (1813–83) was a German composer, director, and conductor. He was primarily known for his operas such as *Tristan and Isolde*, *The Ring of the Nibelung*, and *Parsifal*.

Joseph Viktor Widmann (1842–1911) was a Swiss writer and critic, and editor of the Swiss daily newspaper *Der Bund* from 1880 to 1910.

Ulrich von Wilamowitz-Möllendorff (1848–1931) was a German classical philologist. Primarily known as an authority on ancient Greek literature, he was the dominant classical scholar of his era.

Bernard Williams (1929–2003) was a leading twentieth-century moral philosopher. He opposed the reduction of ethics to abstract systems of rules, and contributed to debates about moral psychology and personal identity.

Ludwig Wittgenstein (1889–1951) is considered by many to be the greatest philosopher of the twentieth century. Best known for his work on logic and his pragmatist theories of meaning, he also contributed to philosophers' understanding of intention and perception, and gave lectures on the foundations of mathematics.

WORKS CITED

WORKS CITED

Benn, Gottfried. "Nietzsche—nach 50 Jahren." In *Nietzsche und die deutsche Literatur*, edited by Bruno Hillebrand. Munich: Deutscher Taschenbuchverlag, 1978.

Bentham, Jeremy. *A Fragment on Government*. New Jersey: The Lawbook Exchange, 2001.

Brobjer, Thomas. *Nietzsche's Philosophical Context: An Intellectual Biography*. Chicago: University of Illinois Press, 2008.

Clarke, Maudemarie. "Nietzsche's Immoralism and the Concept of Morality." In *Nietzsche, Genealogy, Morality: Essays on Nietzsche's Genealogy of Morals*. Edited by Richard Schacht. Berkeley: University of California Press, 1994.

Copleston, Friedrich. *A History of Philosophy*. Vol. 7, *Eighteenth- and Nineteenth-Century German Philosophy*. London: Bloomsbury, 2003.

Craig, Edward. *Knowledge and the State of Nature: An Essay in Conceptual Synthesis*. Oxford: Oxford University Press, 1990.

Deleuze, Gilles. *Nietzsche and Philosophy*. Translated by H. Tomlinson. London: Athlone Press, 1983.

Foot, Philippa. "Nietzsche's Immoralism." In *Nietzsche, Genealogy, Morality: Essays on Nietzsche's Genealogy of Morals*. Edited by Richard Schacht. Berkeley: University of California Press, 1994.

Foucault, Michel. *Discipline and Punish: The Birth of the Prison*. Translated by Alan Sheridan. New York: Pantheon Books, 1977.

___. *History of Madness*. Translated by Jonathan Murphy and Jean Khalfa. Edited by Jean Khalfa. London: Routledge, 2006.

___. *The History of Sexuality*. Vols. 1–3. Translated by Robert Hurley. London: Allen Lane, 1978–86.

___. "Nietzsche, Genealogy, History." In *Language, Counter-Memory, Practice: Selected Essays and Interviews by Michel Foucault*, translated by Donald F. Bouchard and Sherry Simon, edited by Donald F. Bouchard. Oxford: Blackwell, 1977.

___. "Truth, Power, Self: An Interview with Michel Foucault, October 25 1982." In *Technologies of the Self: A Seminar with Michel Foucault*, edited by Luther H. Martin, Huck Gutman, and Patrick H. Hutton, 9–15. London: Tavistock Press, 1988.

Frankena, William K. "Review: MacIntyre and Modern Morality." *Ethics* 93 (1983): 579–87.

Hume, David. *An Enquiry Concerning the Principles of Morals.* Indianapolis: Hackett Publishing Co., 1983.

Janaway, Christopher. *Beyond Selflessness: Reading Nietzsche's* Genealogy. Oxford: Oxford University Press, 2007.

Jones, Ernest. *The Life and Work of Sigmund Freud*. Vols. 1–3. New York: Basic Books, 1953–57.

Kant, Immanuel. *Practical Philosophy*. Translated by Mary Gregor. Cambridge: Cambridge University Press, 1996.

Kaufmann, Walter. *Nietzsche: Philosopher, Psychologist, Antichrist*. New Jersey: Princeton University Press, 1974.

Lange, Friedrich Albert. *The History of Materialism and Criticism of its Present Importance*. Translated by Ernest Chester Thomas. Humanities Press, 1950.

MacIntyre, Alasdair. *After Virtue: A Study in Moral Theory.* London: Bloomsbury, 2011.

Nietzsche, Friedrich. *The Anti-Christ, Ecce Homo, Twilight of the Idols. And Other Writings*. Translated by Judith Norman. Edited by Aaron Ridley. Cambridge: Cambridge University Press, 2005.

____. *Beyond Good and Evil.* Translated by Judith Norman. Edited by Rolf-Peter Horstmann and Judith Norman. Cambridge: Cambridge University Press, 2002.

____. *The Birth of Tragedy and Other Writings*. Translated by Ronald Speirs. Edited by Raymond Geuss and Ronald Speirs. Cambridge: Cambridge University Press, 1999.

____. *Daybreak*. Translated by R. J. Hollingdale. Edited by Maudemarie Clark and Brian Leiter. Cambridge: Cambridge University Press, 1997.

____. *The Gay Science*. Translated by Josefine Nauckhoff. Edited by Bernard Williams. Cambridge: Cambridge University Press, 2001.

____. *Human, All Too Human*. Translated and edited by R. J. Hollingdale. Cambridge: Cambridge University Press, 1996.

____. *On the Genealogy of Morality*. Translated by Maudemarie Clark and Alan Swensen. Indianapolis: Hackett Publishing Co., 1998.

____. *Thus Spoke Zarathustra*. Translated by Adrian Del Caro. Edited by Robert Pippin. Cambridge: Cambridge University Press, 2006.

____. *Untimely Meditations*. Translated by R. J. Hollingdale. Edited by Daniel Breazeale. Cambridge: Cambridge University Press, 1997.

Rée, Paul. *Basic Writings*. Translated and edited by Robin Small. Chicago: University of Illinois Press, 2003.

Safranski, Rüdiger. *Nietzsche: A Philosophical Biography*. Translated by Shelley Frisch. London: Granta Books, 2002.

Sloterdijk, Peter. *Critique of Cynical Reason.* Minnesota: University of Minnesota Press, 1988.

Valente, Joseph. "Beyond Truth and Freedom: The New Faith of Joyce and Nietzsche." *James Joyce Quarterly* 25 (1987): 87–103.

Widmann, Joseph Viktor. "Nietzsche's Dangerous Book." *New Nietzsche Studies* 4 (2000): 195–200.

Williams, Bernard. *Ethics and the Limits of Philosophy*. Abingdon: Routledge, 2011.

____. *Truth and Truthfulness: An Essay in Genealogy.* Princeton: Princeton University Press, 2002.

Wittgenstein, Ludwig. *The Blue and Brown Books*. Oxford: Blackwell, 1958.

____. *Philosophical Investigations*. Translated by P. M. S. Hacker. Edited by Joachim Schulte. Chichester: Wiley-Blackwell, 2009.

THE MACAT LIBRARY
BY DISCIPLINE

AFRICANA STUDIES

Chinua Achebe's *An Image of Africa: Racism in Conrad's Heart of Darkness*
W. E. B. Du Bois's *The Souls of Black Folk*
Zora Neale Huston's *Characteristics of Negro Expression*
Martin Luther King Jr's *Why We Can't Wait*
Toni Morrison's *Playing in the Dark: Whiteness in the American Literary Imagination*

ANTHROPOLOGY

Arjun Appadurai's *Modernity at Large: Cultural Dimensions of Globalisation*
Philippe Ariès's *Centuries of Childhood*
Franz Boas's *Race, Language and Culture*
Kim Chan & Renée Mauborgne's *Blue Ocean Strategy*
Jared Diamond's *Guns, Germs & Steel: the Fate of Human Societies*
Jared Diamond's *Collapse: How Societies Choose to Fail or Survive*
E. E. Evans-Pritchard's *Witchcraft, Oracles and Magic Among the Azande*
James Ferguson's *The Anti-Politics Machine*
Clifford Geertz's *The Interpretation of Cultures*
David Graeber's *Debt: the First 5000 Years*
Karen Ho's *Liquidated: An Ethnography of Wall Street*
Geert Hofstede's *Culture's Consequences: Comparing Values, Behaviors, Institutes and Organizations across Nations*
Claude Lévi-Strauss's *Structural Anthropology*
Jay Macleod's *Ain't No Makin' It: Aspirations and Attainment in a Low-Income Neighborhood*
Saba Mahmood's *The Politics of Piety: The Islamic Revival and the Feminist Subject*
Marcel Mauss's *The Gift*

BUSINESS

Jean Lave & Etienne Wenger's *Situated Learning*
Theodore Levitt's *Marketing Myopia*
Burton G. Malkiel's *A Random Walk Down Wall Street*
Douglas McGregor's *The Human Side of Enterprise*
Michael Porter's *Competitive Strategy: Creating and Sustaining Superior Performance*
John Kotter's *Leading Change*
C. K. Prahalad & Gary Hamel's *The Core Competence of the Corporation*

CRIMINOLOGY

Michelle Alexander's *The New Jim Crow: Mass Incarceration in the Age of Colorblindness*
Michael R. Gottfredson & Travis Hirschi's *A General Theory of Crime*
Richard Herrnstein & Charles A. Murray's *The Bell Curve: Intelligence and Class Structure in American Life*
Elizabeth Loftus's *Eyewitness Testimony*
Jay Macleod's *Ain't No Makin' It: Aspirations and Attainment in a Low-Income Neighborhood*
Philip Zimbardo's *The Lucifer Effect*

ECONOMICS

Janet Abu-Lughod's *Before European Hegemony*
Ha-Joon Chang's *Kicking Away the Ladder*
David Brion Davis's *The Problem of Slavery in the Age of Revolution*
Milton Friedman's *The Role of Monetary Policy*
Milton Friedman's *Capitalism and Freedom*
David Graeber's *Debt: the First 5000 Years*
Friedrich Hayek's *The Road to Serfdom*
Karen Ho's *Liquidated: An Ethnography of Wall Street*

The Macat Library By Discipline

John Maynard Keynes's *The General Theory of Employment, Interest and Money*
Charles P. Kindleberger's *Manias, Panics and Crashes*
Robert Lucas's *Why Doesn't Capital Flow from Rich to Poor Countries?*
Burton G. Malkiel's *A Random Walk Down Wall Street*
Thomas Robert Malthus's *An Essay on the Principle of Population*
Karl Marx's *Capital*
Thomas Piketty's *Capital in the Twenty-First Century*
Amartya Sen's *Development as Freedom*
Adam Smith's *The Wealth of Nations*
Nassim Nicholas Taleb's *The Black Swan: The Impact of the Highly Improbable*
Amos Tversky's & Daniel Kahneman's *Judgment under Uncertainty: Heuristics and Biases*
Mahbub Ul Haq's *Reflections on Human Development*
Max Weber's *The Protestant Ethic and the Spirit of Capitalism*

FEMINISM AND GENDER STUDIES

Judith Butler's *Gender Trouble*
Simone De Beauvoir's *The Second Sex*
Michel Foucault's *History of Sexuality*
Betty Friedan's *The Feminine Mystique*
Saba Mahmood's *The Politics of Piety: The Islamic Revival and the Feminist Subjec*t
Joan Wallach Scott's *Gender and the Politics of History*
Mary Wollstonecraft's *A Vindication of the Rights of Woman*
Virginia Woolf's *A Room of One's Own*

GEOGRAPHY

The Brundtland Report's *Our Common Future*
Rachel Carson's *Silent Spring*
Charles Darwin's *On the Origin of Species*
James Ferguson's *The Anti-Politics Machine*
Jane Jacobs's *The Death and Life of Great American Cities*
James Lovelock's *Gaia: A New Look at Life on Earth*
Amartya Sen's *Development as Freedom*
Mathis Wackernagel & William Rees's *Our Ecological Footprint*

HISTORY

Janet Abu-Lughod's *Before European Hegemony*
Benedict Anderson's *Imagined Communities*
Bernard Bailyn's *The Ideological Origins of the American Revolution*
Hanna Batatu's *The Old Social Classes And The Revolutionary Movements Of Iraq*
Christopher Browning's *Ordinary Men: Reserve Police Batallion 101 and the Final Solution in Poland*
Edmund Burke's *Reflections on the Revolution in France*
William Cronon's *Nature's Metropolis: Chicago And The Great West*
Alfred W. Crosby's *The Columbian Exchange*
Hamid Dabashi's *Iran: A People Interrupted*
David Brion Davis's *The Problem of Slavery in the Age of Revolution*
Nathalie Zemon Davis's *The Return of Martin Guerre*
Jared Diamond's *Guns, Germs & Steel: the Fate of Human Societies*
Frank Dikotter's *Mao's Great Famine*
John W Dower's *War Without Mercy: Race And Power In The Pacific War*
W. E. B. Du Bois's *The Souls of Black Folk*
Richard J. Evans's *In Defence of History*
Lucien Febvre's *The Problem of Unbelief in the 16th Century*
Sheila Fitzpatrick's *Everyday Stalinism*

The Macat Library By Discipline

Eric Foner's *Reconstruction: America's Unfinished Revolution, 1863-1877*
Michel Foucault's *Discipline and Punish*
Michel Foucault's *History of Sexuality*
Francis Fukuyama's *The End of History and the Last Man*
John Lewis Gaddis's *We Now Know: Rethinking Cold War History*
Ernest Gellner's *Nations and Nationalism*
Eugene Genovese's *Roll, Jordan, Roll: The World the Slaves Made*
Carlo Ginzburg's *The Night Battles*
Daniel Goldhagen's *Hitler's Willing Executioners*
Jack Goldstone's *Revolution and Rebellion in the Early Modern World*
Antonio Gramsci's *The Prison Notebooks*
Alexander Hamilton, John Jay & James Madison's *The Federalist Papers*
Christopher Hill's *The World Turned Upside Down*
Carole Hillenbrand's *The Crusades: Islamic Perspectives*
Thomas Hobbes's *Leviathan*
Eric Hobsbawm's *The Age Of Revolution*
John A. Hobson's *Imperialism: A Study*
Albert Hourani's *History of the Arab Peoples*
Samuel P. Huntington's *The Clash of Civilizations and the Remaking of World Order*
C. L. R. James's *The Black Jacobins*
Tony Judt's *Postwar: A History of Europe Since 1945*
Ernst Kantorowicz's *The King's Two Bodies: A Study in Medieval Political Theology*
Paul Kennedy's *The Rise and Fall of the Great Powers*
Ian Kershaw's *The "Hitler Myth": Image and Reality in the Third Reich*
John Maynard Keynes's *The General Theory of Employment, Interest and Money*
Charles P. Kindleberger's *Manias, Panics and Crashes*
Martin Luther King Jr's *Why We Can't Wait*
Henry Kissinger's *World Order: Reflections on the Character of Nations and the Course of History*
Thomas Kuhn's *The Structure of Scientific Revolutions*
Georges Lefebvre's *The Coming of the French Revolution*
John Locke's *Two Treatises of Government*
Niccolò Machiavelli's *The Prince*
Thomas Robert Malthus's *An Essay on the Principle of Population*
Mahmood Mamdani's *Citizen and Subject: Contemporary Africa And The Legacy Of Late Colonialism*
Karl Marx's *Capital*
Stanley Milgram's *Obedience to Authority*
John Stuart Mill's *On Liberty*
Thomas Paine's *Common Sense*
Thomas Paine's *Rights of Man*
Geoffrey Parker's *Global Crisis: War, Climate Change and Catastrophe in the Seventeenth Century*
Jonathan Riley-Smith's *The First Crusade and the Idea of Crusading*
Jean-Jacques Rousseau's *The Social Contract*
Joan Wallach Scott's *Gender and the Politics of History*
Theda Skocpol's *States and Social Revolutions*
Adam Smith's *The Wealth of Nations*
Timothy Snyder's *Bloodlands: Europe Between Hitler and Stalin*
Sun Tzu's *The Art of War*
Keith Thomas's *Religion and the Decline of Magic*
Thucydides's *The History of the Peloponnesian War*
Frederick Jackson Turner's *The Significance of the Frontier in American History*
Odd Arne Westad's *The Global Cold War: Third World Interventions And The Making Of Our Times*

LITERATURE

Chinua Achebe's *An Image of Africa: Racism in Conrad's Heart of Darkness*
Roland Barthes's *Mythologies*
Homi K. Bhabha's *The Location of Culture*
Judith Butler's *Gender Trouble*
Simone De Beauvoir's *The Second Sex*
Ferdinand De Saussure's *Course in General Linguistics*
T. S. Eliot's *The Sacred Wood: Essays on Poetry and Criticism*
Zora Neale Huston's *Characteristics of Negro Expression*
Toni Morrison's *Playing in the Dark: Whiteness in the American Literary Imagination*
Edward Said's *Orientalism*
Gayatri Chakravorty Spivak's *Can the Subaltern Speak?*
Mary Wollstonecraft's *A Vindication of the Rights of Women*
Virginia Woolf's *A Room of One's Own*

PHILOSOPHY

Elizabeth Anscombe's *Modern Moral Philosophy*
Hannah Arendt's *The Human Condition*
Aristotle's *Metaphysics*
Aristotle's *Nicomachean Ethics*
Edmund Gettier's *Is Justified True Belief Knowledge?*
Georg Wilhelm Friedrich Hegel's *Phenomenology of Spirit*
David Hume's *Dialogues Concerning Natural Religion*
David Hume's *The Enquiry for Human Understanding*
Immanuel Kant's *Religion within the Boundaries of Mere Reason*
Immanuel Kant's *Critique of Pure Reason*
Søren Kierkegaard's *The Sickness Unto Death*
Søren Kierkegaard's *Fear and Trembling*
C. S. Lewis's *The Abolition of Man*
Alasdair MacIntyre's *After Virtue*
Marcus Aurelius's *Meditations*
Friedrich Nietzsche's *On the Genealogy of Morality*
Friedrich Nietzsche's *Beyond Good and Evil*
Plato's *Republic*
Plato's *Symposium*
Jean-Jacques Rousseau's *The Social Contract*
Gilbert Ryle's *The Concept of Mind*
Baruch Spinoza's *Ethics*
Sun Tzu's *The Art of War*
Ludwig Wittgenstein's *Philosophical Investigations*

POLITICS

Benedict Anderson's *Imagined Communities*
Aristotle's *Politics*
Bernard Bailyn's *The Ideological Origins of the American Revolution*
Edmund Burke's *Reflections on the Revolution in France*
John C. Calhoun's *A Disquisition on Government*
Ha-Joon Chang's *Kicking Away the Ladder*
Hamid Dabashi's *Iran: A People Interrupted*
Hamid Dabashi's *Theology of Discontent: The Ideological Foundation of the Islamic Revolution in Iran*
Robert Dahl's *Democracy and its Critics*
Robert Dahl's *Who Governs?*
David Brion Davis's *The Problem of Slavery in the Age of Revolution*

Alexis De Tocqueville's *Democracy in America*
James Ferguson's *The Anti-Politics Machine*
Frank Dikotter's *Mao's Great Famine*
Sheila Fitzpatrick's *Everyday Stalinism*
Eric Foner's *Reconstruction: America's Unfinished Revolution, 1863-1877*
Milton Friedman's *Capitalism and Freedom*
Francis Fukuyama's *The End of History and the Last Man*
John Lewis Gaddis's *We Now Know: Rethinking Cold War History*
Ernest Gellner's *Nations and Nationalism*
David Graeber's *Debt: the First 5000 Years*
Antonio Gramsci's *The Prison Notebooks*
Alexander Hamilton, John Jay & James Madison's *The Federalist Papers*
Friedrich Hayek's *The Road to Serfdom*
Christopher Hill's *The World Turned Upside Down*
Thomas Hobbes's *Leviathan*
John A. Hobson's *Imperialism: A Study*
Samuel P. Huntington's *The Clash of Civilizations and the Remaking of World Order*
Tony Judt's *Postwar: A History of Europe Since 1945*
David C. Kang's *China Rising: Peace, Power and Order in East Asia*
Paul Kennedy's *The Rise and Fall of Great Powers*
Robert Keohane's *After Hegemony*
Martin Luther King Jr.'s *Why We Can't Wait*
Henry Kissinger's *World Order: Reflections on the Character of Nations and the Course of History*
John Locke's *Two Treatises of Government*
Niccolò Machiavelli's *The Prince*
Thomas Robert Malthus's *An Essay on the Principle of Population*
Mahmood Mamdani's *Citizen and Subject: Contemporary Africa And The Legacy Of Late Colonialism*
Karl Marx's *Capital*
John Stuart Mill's *On Liberty*
John Stuart Mill's *Utilitarianism*
Hans Morgenthau's *Politics Among Nations*
Thomas Paine's *Common Sense*
Thomas Paine's *Rights of Man*
Thomas Piketty's *Capital in the Twenty-First Century*
Robert D. Putnam's *Bowling Alone*
John Rawls's *Theory of Justice*
Jean-Jacques Rousseau's *The Social Contract*
Theda Skocpol's *States and Social Revolutions*
Adam Smith's *The Wealth of Nations*
Sun Tzu's *The Art of War*
Henry David Thoreau's *Civil Disobedience*
Thucydides's *The History of the Peloponnesian War*
Kenneth Waltz's *Theory of International Politics*
Max Weber's *Politics as a Vocation*
Odd Arne Westad's *The Global Cold War: Third World Interventions And The Making Of Our Times*

POSTCOLONIAL STUDIES

Roland Barthes's *Mythologies*
Frantz Fanon's *Black Skin, White Masks*
Homi K. Bhabha's *The Location of Culture*
Gustavo Gutiérrez's *A Theology of Liberation*
Edward Said's *Orientalism*
Gayatri Chakravorty Spivak's *Can the Subaltern Speak?*

The Macat Library By Discipline

PSYCHOLOGY

Gordon Allport's *The Nature of Prejudice*
Alan Baddeley & Graham Hitch's *Aggression: A Social Learning Analysis*
Albert Bandura's *Aggression: A Social Learning Analysis*
Leon Festinger's *A Theory of Cognitive Dissonance*
Sigmund Freud's *The Interpretation of Dreams*
Betty Friedan's *The Feminine Mystique*
Michael R. Gottfredson & Travis Hirschi's *A General Theory of Crime*
Eric Hoffer's *The True Believer: Thoughts on the Nature of Mass Movements*
William James's *Principles of Psychology*
Elizabeth Loftus's *Eyewitness Testimony*
A. H. Maslow's *A Theory of Human Motivation*
Stanley Milgram's *Obedience to Authority*
Steven Pinker's *The Better Angels of Our Nature*
Oliver Sacks's *The Man Who Mistook His Wife For a Hat*
Richard Thaler & Cass Sunstein's *Nudge: Improving Decisions About Health, Wealth and Happiness*
Amos Tversky's *Judgment under Uncertainty: Heuristics and Biases*
Philip Zimbardo's *The Lucifer Effect*

SCIENCE

Rachel Carson's *Silent Spring*
William Cronon's *Nature's Metropolis: Chicago And The Great West*
Alfred W. Crosby's *The Columbian Exchange*
Charles Darwin's *On the Origin of Species*
Richard Dawkin's *The Selfish Gene*
Thomas Kuhn's *The Structure of Scientific Revolutions*
Geoffrey Parker's *Global Crisis: War, Climate Change and Catastrophe in the Seventeenth Century*
Mathis Wackernagel & William Rees's *Our Ecological Footprint*

SOCIOLOGY

Michelle Alexander's *The New Jim Crow: Mass Incarceration in the Age of Colorblindness*
Gordon Allport's *The Nature of Prejudice*
Albert Bandura's *Aggression: A Social Learning Analysis*
Hanna Batatu's *The Old Social Classes And The Revolutionary Movements Of Iraq*
Ha-Joon Chang's *Kicking Away the Ladder*
W. E. B. Du Bois's *The Souls of Black Folk*
Émile Durkheim's *On Suicide*
Frantz Fanon's *Black Skin, White Masks*
Frantz Fanon's *The Wretched of the Earth*
Eric Foner's *Reconstruction: America's Unfinished Revolution, 1863-1877*
Eugene Genovese's *Roll, Jordan, Roll: The World the Slaves Made*
Jack Goldstone's *Revolution and Rebellion in the Early Modern World*
Antonio Gramsci's *The Prison Notebooks*
Richard Herrnstein & Charles A Murray's *The Bell Curve: Intelligence and Class Structure in American Life*
Eric Hoffer's *The True Believer: Thoughts on the Nature of Mass Movements*
Jane Jacobs's *The Death and Life of Great American Cities*
Robert Lucas's *Why Doesn't Capital Flow from Rich to Poor Countries?*
Jay Macleod's *Ain't No Makin' It: Aspirations and Attainment in a Low Income Neighborhood*
Elaine May's *Homeward Bound: American Families in the Cold War Era*
Douglas McGregor's *The Human Side of Enterprise*
C. Wright Mills's *The Sociological Imagination*

Thomas Piketty's *Capital in the Twenty-First Century*
Robert D. Putman's *Bowling Alone*
David Riesman's *The Lonely Crowd: A Study of the Changing American Character*
Edward Said's *Orientalism*
Joan Wallach Scott's *Gender and the Politics of History*
Theda Skocpol's *States and Social Revolutions*
Max Weber's *The Protestant Ethic and the Spirit of Capitalism*

THEOLOGY

Augustine's *Confessions*
Benedict's *Rule of St Benedict*
Gustavo Gutiérrez's *A Theology of Liberation*
Carole Hillenbrand's *The Crusades: Islamic Perspectives*
David Hume's *Dialogues Concerning Natural Religion*
Immanuel Kant's *Religion within the Boundaries of Mere Reason*
Ernst Kantorowicz's *The King's Two Bodies: A Study in Medieval Political Theology*
Søren Kierkegaard's *The Sickness Unto Death*
C. S. Lewis's *The Abolition of Man*
Saba Mahmood's *The Politics of Piety: The Islamic Revival and the Feminist Subject*
Baruch Spinoza's *Ethics*
Keith Thomas's *Religion and the Decline of Magic*

COMING SOON

Chris Argyris's *The Individual and the Organisation*
Seyla Benhabib's *The Rights of Others*
Walter Benjamin's *The Work Of Art in the Age of Mechanical Reproduction*
John Berger's *Ways of Seeing*
Pierre Bourdieu's *Outline of a Theory of Practice*
Mary Douglas's *Purity and Danger*
Roland Dworkin's *Taking Rights Seriously*
James G. March's *Exploration and Exploitation in Organisational Learning*
Ikujiro Nonaka's *A Dynamic Theory of Organizational Knowledge Creation*
Griselda Pollock's *Vision and Difference*
Amartya Sen's *Inequality Re-Examined*
Susan Sontag's *On Photography*
Yasser Tabbaa's *The Transformation of Islamic Art*
Ludwig von Mises's *Theory of Money and Credit*

The Macat Library By Discipline

The Macat Library By Discipline

Assess the greatest ideas and thinkers
across entire disciplines, including

MACAT

Roland Barthes's Mythologies
Frantz Fanon's Black Skin, White Masks
Homi K. Bhabha's The Location of Culture
Gustavo Gutiérrez's A Theology of Liberation
Edward Said's Orientalism
Gayatri Chakravorty Spivak's Can the Subaltern Speak?

Macat analyses are available from all good bookshops and libraries.
Access hundreds of analyses through one, multimedia tool.
Join free for one month library.macat.com

Macat Disciplines

Access the greatest ideas and thinkers across entire disciplines, including

Postcolonial Studies

Roland Barthes's *Mythologies*
Frantz Fanon's *Black Skin, White Masks*
Homi K. Bhabha's *The Location of Culture*
Gustavo Gutiérrez's *A Theology of Liberation*
Edward Said's *Orientalism*
Gayatri Chakravorty Spivak's *Can the Subaltern Speak?*

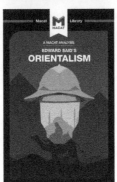

Macat analyses are available from all good bookshops and libraries.

Access hundreds of analyses through one, multimedia tool.
Join free for one month **library.macat.com**

Macat Disciplines

*Access the greatest ideas and thinkers
across entire disciplines, including*

FEMINISM, GENDER AND QUEER STUDIES

Simone De Beauvoir's
The Second Sex

Michel Foucault's
History of Sexuality

Betty Friedan's
The Feminine Mystique

Saba Mahmood's
*The Politics of Piety:
The Islamic Revival and
the Feminist Subject*

Joan Wallach Scott's
*Gender and the
Politics of History*

Mary Wollstonecraft's
*A Vindication of the
Rights of Woman*

Virginia Woolf's
A Room of One's Own

Judith Butler's
Gender Trouble

Macat Disciplines

Access the greatest ideas and thinkers across entire disciplines, including

CRIMINOLOGY

Michelle Alexander's
The New Jim Crow: Mass Incarceration in the Age of Colorblindness

Michael R. Gottfredson & Travis Hirschi's
A General Theory of Crime

Elizabeth Loftus's
Eyewitness Testimony

Richard Herrnstein & Charles A. Murray's
The Bell Curve: Intelligence and Class Structure in American Life

Jay Macleod's
Ain't No Makin' It: Aspirations and Attainment in a Low-Income Neighborhood

Philip Zimbardo's
The Lucifer Effect

Macat Disciplines

Access the greatest ideas and thinkers across entire disciplines, including

INEQUALITY

Ha-Joon Chang's, *Kicking Away the Ladder*

David Graeber's, *Debt: The First 5000 Years*

Robert E. Lucas's, *Why Doesn't Capital Flow from Rich To Poor Countries?*

Thomas Piketty's, *Capital in the Twenty-First Century*

Amartya Sen's, *Inequality Re-Examined*

Mahbub Ul Haq's, *Reflections on Human Development*

  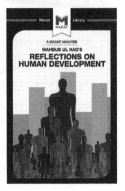

Macat analyses are available from all good bookshops and libraries.

Access hundreds of analyses through one, multimedia tool.
Join free for one month **library.macat.com**

Macat Disciplines

Access the greatest ideas and thinkers across entire disciplines, including

GLOBALIZATION

Arjun Appadurai's, *Modernity at Large: Cultural Dimensions of Globalisation*

James Ferguson's, *The Anti-Politics Machine*

Geert Hofstede's, *Culture's Consequences*

Amartya Sen's, *Development as Freedom*

Macat analyses are available from all good bookshops and libraries.

Access hundreds of analyses through one, multimedia tool.
Join free for one month **library.macat.com**

Macat Disciplines

Access the greatest ideas and thinkers across entire disciplines, including

MAN AND THE ENVIRONMENT

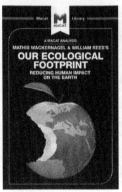

The Brundtland Report's, *Our Common Future*
Rachel Carson's, *Silent Spring*
James Lovelock's, *Gaia: A New Look at Life on Earth*
Mathis Wackernagel & William Rees's, *Our Ecological Footprint*

Macat analyses are available from all good bookshops and libraries.

Access hundreds of analyses through one, multimedia tool.
Join free for one month **library.macat.com**

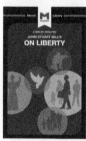

Macat Disciplines

Access the greatest ideas and thinkers across entire disciplines, including

TOTALITARIANISM

Sheila Fitzpatrick's, *Everyday Stalinism*
Ian Kershaw's, *The "Hitler Myth"*
Timothy Snyder's, *Bloodlands*

Macat Pairs

Analyse historical and modern issues from opposite sides of an argument. Pairs include:

RACE AND IDENTITY

Zora Neale Hurston's
Characteristics of Negro Expression

Using material collected on anthropological expeditions to the South, Zora Neale Hurston explains how expression in African American culture in the early twentieth century departs from the art of white America. At the time, African American art was often criticized for copying white culture. For Hurston, this criticism misunderstood how art works. European tradition views art as something fixed. But Hurston describes a creative process that is alive, ever-changing, and largely improvisational. She maintains that African American art works through a process called 'mimicry'—where an imitated object or verbal pattern, for example, is reshaped and altered until it becomes something new, novel—and worthy of attention.

Frantz Fanon's
Black Skin, White Masks

Black Skin, White Masks offers a radical analysis of the psychological effects of colonization on the colonized.

Fanon witnessed the effects of colonization first hand both in his birthplace, Martinique, and again later in life when he worked as a psychiatrist in another French colony, Algeria. His text is uncompromising in form and argument. He dissects the dehumanizing effects of colonialism, arguing that it destroys the native sense of identity, forcing people to adapt to an alien set of values—including a core belief that they are inferior. This results in deep psychological trauma.

Fanon's work played a pivotal role in the civil rights movements of the 1960s.

Macat analyses are available from all good bookshops and libraries.

Access hundreds of analyses through one, multimedia tool.
Join free for one month **library.macat.com**

Macat Pairs

*Analyse historical and modern issues
from opposite sides of an argument.
Pairs include:*

INTERNATIONAL RELATIONS IN THE 21ST CENTURY

Samuel P. Huntington's
The Clash of Civilisations

In his highly influential 1996 book, Huntington offers a vision of a post-Cold War world in which conflict takes place not between competing ideologies but between cultures. The worst clash, he argues, will be between the Islamic world and the West: the West's arrogance and belief that its culture is a "gift" to the world will come into conflict with Islam's obstinacy and concern that its culture is under attack from a morally decadent "other."

Clash inspired much debate between different political schools of thought. But its greatest impact came in helping define American foreign policy in the wake of the 2001 terrorist attacks in New York and Washington.

Francis Fukuyama's
The End of History and the Last Man

Published in 1992, *The End of History and the Last Man* argues that capitalist democracy is the final destination for all societies. Fukuyama believed democracy triumphed during the Cold War because it lacks the "fundamental contradictions" inherent in communism and satisfies our yearning for freedom and equality. Democracy therefore marks the endpoint in the evolution of ideology, and so the "end of history." There will still be "events," but no fundamental change in ideology.

Macat Pairs

*Analyse historical and modern issues
from opposite sides of an argument.
Pairs include:*

HOW TO RUN AN ECONOMY

John Maynard Keynes's
*The General Theory OF Employment,
Interest and Money*

Classical economics suggests that market economies are self-correcting in times of recession or depression, and tend toward full employment and output. But English economist John Maynard Keynes disagrees.

In his ground-breaking 1936 study *The General Theory*, Keynes argues that traditional economics has misunderstood the causes of unemployment. Employment is not determined by the price of labor; it is directly linked to demand. Keynes believes market economies are by nature unstable, and so require government intervention. Spurred on by the social catastrophe of the Great Depression of the 1930s, he sets out to revolutionize the way the world thinks

Milton Friedman's
The Role of Monetary Policy

Friedman's 1968 paper changed the course of economic theory. In just 17 pages, he demolished existing theory and outlined an effective alternate monetary policy designed to secure 'high employment, stable prices and rapid growth.'

Friedman demonstrated that monetary policy plays a vital role in broader economic stability and argued that economists got their monetary policy wrong in the 1950s and 1960s by misunderstanding the relationship between inflation and unemployment. Previous generations of economists had believed that governments could permanently decrease unemployment by permitting inflation—and vice versa. Friedman's most original contribution was to show that this supposed trade-off is an illusion that only works in the short term.

Macat analyses are available from all good bookshops and libraries.

Access hundreds of analyses through one, multimedia tool.
Join free for one month **library.macat.com**

Macat Pairs

Analyse historical and modern issues from opposite sides of an argument. Pairs include:

ARE WE FUNDAMENTALLY GOOD - OR BAD?

Steven Pinker's
The Better Angels of Our Nature

Stephen Pinker's gloriously optimistic 2011 book argues that, despite humanity's biological tendency toward violence, we are, in fact, less violent today than ever before. To prove his case, Pinker lays out pages of detailed statistical evidence. For him, much of the credit for the decline goes to the eighteenth-century Enlightenment movement, whose ideas of liberty, tolerance, and respect for the value of human life filtered down through society and affected how people thought. That psychological change led to behavioral change—and overall we became more peaceful. Critics countered that humanity could never overcome the biological urge toward violence; others argued that Pinker's statistics were flawed.

Philip Zimbardo's
The Lucifer Effect

Some psychologists believe those who commit cruelty are innately evil. Zimbardo disagrees. In *The Lucifer Effect*, he argues that sometimes good people do evil things simply because of the situations they find themselves in, citing many historical examples to illustrate his point. Zimbardo details his 1971 Stanford prison experiment, where ordinary volunteers playing guards in a mock prison rapidly became abusive. But he also describes the tortures committed by US army personnel in Iraq's Abu Ghraib prison in 2003—and how he himself testified in defence of one of those guards. committed by US army personnel in Iraq's Abu Ghraib prison in 2003—and how he himself testified in defence of one of those guards.

Macat Pairs

Analyse historical and modern issues from opposite sides of an argument. Pairs include:

HOW WE RELATE TO EACH OTHER AND SOCIETY

Jean-Jacques Rousseau's
The Social Contract

Rousseau's famous work sets out the radical concept of the 'social contract': a give-and-take relationship between individual freedom and social order.

If people are free to do as they like, governed only by their own sense of justice, they are also vulnerable to chaos and violence. To avoid this, Rousseau proposes, they should agree to give up some freedom to benefit from the protection of social and political organization. But this deal is only just if societies are led by the collective needs and desires of the people, and able to control the private interests of individuals. For Rousseau, the only legitimate form of government is rule by the people.

Robert D. Putnam's
Bowling Alone

In *Bowling Alone*, Robert Putnam argues that Americans have become disconnected from one another and from the institutions of their common life, and investigates the consequences of this change.

Looking at a range of indicators, from membership in formal organizations to the number of invitations being extended to informal dinner parties, Putnam demonstrates that Americans are interacting less and creating less "social capital" – with potentially disastrous implications for their society.

It would be difficult to overstate the impact of *Bowling Alone*, one of the most frequently cited social science publications of the last half-century.

For Product Safety Concerns and Information please contact our EU
representative GPSR@taylorandfrancis.com Taylor & Francis Verlag GmbH,
Kaufingerstraße 24, 80331 München, Germany

Printed and bound by CPI Group (UK) Ltd, Croydon, CR0 4YY
08/06/2025
01896977-0003